CAN'T LOSE

14 WINNING WEIGHT-LOSS SECRETS FOR WOMEN WHO THINK THEY CAN'T LOSE WEIGHT

DAVE SMITH

CAN'T LOSE

14 WINNING WEIGHT-LOSS SECRETS FOR WOMEN WHO <u>THINK</u> THEY CAN'T LOSE WEIGHT

ACKNOWLEDGEMENTS

I would like to first thank the 14 health professionals who were interviewed for this book. You dedicate your careers and your lives to helping others live well. Your passion for healthy living makes the world a much better place.

I would also like to thank all of you who listen to my Make Your Body Work podcast, especially those who have written in with your questions about weight-loss and healthy living. Without you opening up and sharing your life with me, there would be no podcast, the interviews you're about to read would not have taken place, and this book and its accompanying resources would not exist.

Thank you for letting me be part of your life journey. You inspire me to keep doing what I do.

TABLE OF CONTENTS

INTRODUCTION

I attended a college in Pensacola, Florida that had a unique rule: each semester, every single student had to enroll in one physical education class. Students could choose any PE class they wanted, whether it be basketball, swimming, track, or something else, but every student had to participate.

Another rule: part of a student's grade in their PE course was directly derived from their athletic performance. Be athletic, and you get a good grade – it wasn't exactly the fairest grading system imaginable.

On my first day in the "Physical Fitness" class, I met Patrick. He was likable from the get-go. He cracked jokes, made an effort to get to know each of our classmates, and he had a thick Texan accent that was intriguing, and a little comical, to a Canadian like me (He spent plenty of time making fun of my "oot's" and "aboot's" so I can pick on his southern drawl, right?).

Patrick weighed about 300 pounds.

That semester there were many times when my heart broke for Patrick. He struggled to jog for more than a minute or two. He couldn't do push-ups let alone the rope climb we practiced each week. And during evaluation time, Patrick always scored the lowest of anyone in our class.

Although he never said so, I can't imagine that Patrick enjoyed the class one bit. In fact, I wouldn't be surprised if he grew to hate "Physical Fitness" altogether.

Fast-forward nearly twenty years, and I can tell you that I've met thousands of "Patricks" – these are the people who are told that health and fitness have to look a certain way.

"If you can't run, or if you don't like going to the gym, then you can't exercise."

"If you don't eat low-fat, low-carb, Paleo, gluten-free, organic, or [insert any other diet of the day], then you're not a healthy eater."

The number of people who've given up on health, fitness, or weight-loss because they can't live up to what someone else tells them to do is greater than I can count.

So, before you read one more page in this book, I want you to know the most important truth when it comes to healthy living:

You are unique.

Your healthy life is going to be a unique one. There *is* a way that you can enjoy exercise. There *is* a way that you can eat a healthy diet. There *is* a way you can lose weight, keep it off, and feel great about your body. Your unique path to a healthy life does exist, and it's not going to look like anyone else's.

I haven't seen Patrick in nearly 20 years, so I can only hope that he's figured this out along the way. I hope he didn't decide that healthy living or fitness isn't for him simply because he was taught it had to look a certain way.

That's why I wrote this book.

I'm not going to tell you how I stay healthy. Nobody needs another book outlining a "perfect" selection of recipes or exercise routines that some fitness expert claims to use. No, you don't need to do what I do.

Instead, this book brings together 14 interviews I conducted with some of the top health and fitness experts in the world. These health professionals have helped millions of people get in better shape, and they are here to answer specific questions from people just like you. These questions are about losing weight, gaining energy, becoming more physically fit, loving your body, and feeling successful.

The secrets shared by the experts you're about to meet will become pieces to your unique weight-loss puzzle. How you put these pieces together will be different from anyone else, but let me assure you that your solution is available in the interviews you're about to read. Your unique path begins here.

Before you dive in, there are two things you must keep in mind:

    1. It's impossible to do everything at once.

    2. You can begin today.

You are going to be inspired as you read this book. And, as you feel more and more inspired, it can be tempting to act on everything you learn. After all, if these strategies work, why not implement them as soon as possible?

Please resist that temptation.

Doing everything is only sustainable for so long, and it almost always leads to burnout, frustration, and a feeling of failure. I don't want that for you.

Instead, try to identify one "golden nugget" from each interview. What's that one thing that will make the biggest impact in your life?

Then, it's time to start. It's time to put that golden nugget into practice. Accumulating more information about getting in shape isn't all that helpful on its own. Action is required.

If you're using the workbook that accompanies this book, you'll find all sorts of guidance to accomplish this. I'll lead you through the baby steps required for real, lasting change. If you don't have the workbook, feel free to contact me for help: dave@makeyourbodywork.com.

Your friend and fitness coach,

Dave Smith

PS - You'll find many resources linked to in this book. All links are working as of the printing of this book, but they could change over time. If this happens, I'll do my best to update them in future editions of this book.

CHAPTER 1:

IS A "HEALTHY LIFESTYLE" REALLY POSSIBLE?

If you just want to lose weight, you can skip reading the rest of this book and follow an equation that will likely get you there:

Eat less. Exercise more.

Simple, right?

Take in fewer calories each day, while expending a couple more, and surely you'll begin to lose weight.

But, if weight-loss were so simple, there would be no books like this one you're reading right now. There would be no diet plans. There wouldn't be slimming supplements. And health coaches like me would be out of a job!

Eating less and exercising more sounds easy, but it isn't. Your body (and your life) is far too complex to throw such a simplistic solution at a very multifaceted problem.

That's why crash dieting and extreme exercise have come under fire lately. Informed consumers have realized that diets and workout programs have been around for decades, but the battle against obesity isn't being won.

Hence why there is a trendy statement to make these days: "Forget dieting. Just create a healthy lifestyle," and apparently all your health and fitness goals will magically fall into place without much effort.

Make it a lifestyle.

It sounds great, but in practice, how does this work for someone whose lifestyle isn't as healthy as they'd like?

That's the question Sadie posed:

> *"I hear this message all the time, 'Make it a lifestyle.' I understand that it would be ideal to make healthy choices a lifestyle and not a daily grind, but for me, I don't ever see my life becoming a breeze of healthy choices.*

I don't mean to be negative, I will continue to strive to be better, but sometimes I think that this elusive, 'healthy lifestyle' really is just out of reach for most of us."

Can you create a healthy lifestyle that makes weight-loss feel like less of a grind? Is it realistic to think that you can foster a lifestyle that feels natural and gets you the results you want?

MEET MELISSA KATHRYN

Melissa Kathryn is a weight-loss and lifestyle expert who owns a self-named company dedicated to changing the lives of women by helping them reclaim control over their bodies.

She has been an influential TED talk presenter, has appeared on numerous television shows, and writes for a variety of health and fitness publications.

THE INTERVIEW

Dave: Hey, Melissa, thanks so much for being a part of this interview today.

Melissa: Thanks so much for having me. This is so fun.

Dave: Yeah, you and I recently met because I am a guest in your upcoming summit. Do you want to tell us quickly about that summit?

Melissa: Yeah, and I loved our interview. Thank you for being a part of that. It is called *Done with Dieting*, and it is the number one online event to lose weight, stop dieting and emotional eating, and to love your body now.

My mission is to free people from dieting, to help them learn how to lose weight effortlessly and reconnect with food. To build and heal that relationship. To make peace with food and make peace with themselves, so they really thrive in life with a body they love.

The summit was super kickass and spoke to that and gave people a lot of great, not only guidance, but actionable tips. I'm big on getting results and putting things into action right away. That's what you and the other speakers provided for the audience. I was really proud and just super grateful to have been able to create something free like that for everybody.

Dave: Yeah, you know what else is cool, is I was looking at your professional bio page, and you have some really interesting pictures. It shows you in the state you call emotional eating, a picture of you when you were in your dieting phase, and then you in your healthy and happy phase. It's really cool because when I look at your dieter phase, in particular, you're in a swimsuit. You must have been getting ready for some competition?

Melissa: Yeah, I was a fitness competitor. I won best body division in the International Natural Body Federation.

Dave: I love the fact that you have that labeled as a dieter. And maybe you can tell the readers, what did you think about your health at that stage?

THE DIETER'S PRISON

Melissa: It's so funny that you asked me that today. You and I both know there are always so many facets to our story, but we end up just sharing the same piece.

It's like my story is almost split into these three areas. You see it in those pictures, so when you guys go to my Facebook fan page, you'll see it, and you can click on it and blow it up. You'll see what I'm talking about.

Yeah, at that point in time, I was a fitness expert, a trainer, and I knew how to transform any body. I knew the science behind it. Then, I was a certified holistic nutritionist and health coach. I knew all of these things, and yet I was in what I call a dieter's prison. From the outside, everyone's just like, "Oh, Melissa's just so healthy." Now they actually have a term for it.

I was on the phone with one of my friends—an amazing psychiatrist out of New York City and she was on Done with Dieting—Terri Cole. She said there's a term now for the dieter where you are uber healthy, you don't eat gluten, don't eat dairy, and don't have bread. You have three food groups like vegetables and water. Water's not a food group, but you get what I'm saying.

Dave: Yeah, totally.

Melissa: For some people, it's kind of scary. It's like models with their orange juice and cotton balls. If you don't know what I'm talking about...

Dave: I was going to ask you because I have no idea. What are orange juice and cotton balls for?

Melissa: Models will actually eat cotton balls dipped in orange juice to get the nutrients of the orange juice, but the cotton expands in their stomach, that way they don't eat.

Dave: Okay, that sounds extremely unhealthy.

Melissa: Yes. To go back to what you were talking about, at that time I didn't understand. There was a pivotal point for me after I won best body and got a ginormous trophy (almost the size of me, it's the biggest thing I've ever, I was like "Oh, my god!"). I gained the weight back in six months. I think it was closer to three because I sabotaged myself since I was still emotionally tied to food. I would binge, but I would binge on health foods.

That's what happens when you come out of training like that. I was introduced to all of these fake foods like protein powders and protein bars that mimic candy bars. I thought I was an ex-emotional eater, but it was still there because I never really got to the root of it. I just moved from one thing to another. I went from an emotional eater to an extreme dieter. Both filled with deprivation and all coming from a lack of love for myself and a feeling of being not deserving. Not enough. Not worthy.

For me, I felt worthy when I was at a certain weight. But after getting to that weight, I never really enjoyed it or saw myself there because I was so worried I wouldn't stay there. Everything I did was about how I could stay there. Friends would say, "Hey, Melissa, do you want to come and watch football with us on a Sunday?" And I was like no. Oh, my god, I'll be around all bar food. What, am I going to bring my own food? But then I'll deviate from my diet, and I need to get up for the gym in the morning. So, I'm going to go home and make a healthy meal and sit by myself, so devoid of fun.

To answer your question, at that time, I thought I was like everybody else because I was like everyone else that stood on that stage. I thought that was a normal way to be. What really happened was I had such an unhealthy relationship with food. If I had a good day or a bad day, everything related back. Like I said, it was a dieter's prison. Getting out of that is what I teach people to do now so they can actually enjoy their body.

You know, when you talk to people and they say, "I don't know why I thought I was fat because I look back on pictures and I look damned good." It's like yeah, wouldn't it be great if you would have actually saw yourself the way you were?

Dave: Yeah, it's so interesting.

Melissa: You would have saved yourself a lot of pain, a lot of money, and you would have had a hell of a lot more fun.

WHAT'S THE "PINNACLE OF FITNESS" REALLY LIKE?

Dave: I love the fact that you're open and honest about your own story because I just love people who have been in the industry and thought themselves to be at the pinnacle of fitness. When you look at your pictures, you can tell you're in competition, and it sounds like you won the competition. So, obviously, you're the pinnacle of fitness. But you, in your own words, say it wasn't healthy; it wasn't fun.

It sounds like it was isolating, it put you in a bad psychological space, and that's the message. We haven't even gotten into the question for today, but to all the readers, that's a message I want you to hold onto. You shouldn't be striving for what you see portrayed in the media as being the "pinnacle of fitness" because it's not fitness. It's not healthy.

Melissa: Yeah, for anybody that wants to do a competition, it can be a great experience. It was for me in a lot of ways, and it was also very eye-opening, it's what led me here.

I really want to address that when you see a fitness model—men and women—they are in that shape because they live that way day in and day out. They've got four hours a day in the gym. They're walking around with a cooler bag and their food. There's nothing wrong with that. I still walk around with food.

I just went to a conference, and I live what I teach. I know how to eat for my body. I like healthy food. I eat clean. I went there with sweet potatoes in a bag and cucumber sticks. I was pulling them out like they were apples. I brought my own oatmeal with protein powder in it and fruit, and I just added water, and I cooked it in my room.

I do those things because I like to rely on myself and to know what I'm putting in my body. But I'm also not afraid if I don't have them on me. I'm not in fear of what that will do to me, but certain things have become my lifestyle. You really want to get clear with yourself on what can you maintain for life. What is going to fuel you, make you happy, and give you a life at the same time?

Dave: This is awesome. Everything that we're talking about right now is so tied into Sadie's question. You even use the word a few seconds ago, lifestyle. She says, "Dave, everyone talks about making a healthy lifestyle." Make it a lifestyle.

She says, "I hear this everywhere, but for me, I don't ever see my life becoming a breeze of healthy choices." What do you say to someone like Sadie who just doesn't feel like it'll ever become a lifestyle for her?

How Can You Change Your Mindset?

Melissa: First off, Sadie, you have to change your mindset because that's where all of this starts. When I said I gained the weight back, I easily could have dug myself into a hole. I'm a health coach, and you just saw me transform my body one way and eat it back within a millisecond. I could have sat there and said, "I will never get where I want to be."

What I tell people when we're going to make it a lifestyle is to shift your thinking to what you're gaining instead of what you're giving up. Start to identify who you want to be. The person that you want to be is the person that's reading this book, or you wouldn't be here.

I just came off of running my Weight-Loss for Life Retreat, and an exercise that I have all of the women do there was, I said, "I want you to write down who you are." The theme of the retreat was "I am her, I'm already the woman," meaning you're already the woman that you want to be, you just need to believe that. Then the rest will show up for you and be created around you.

Right now, you're in resistance to her, so there's a conflict. I say I want one thing, but I'm doing another. When we want to start to embrace something as a lifestyle, take small steps instead of doing an all or nothing. I tell people to live in the rainbow in between. Instead of the black or white, live in the rainbow and take baby steps to get there. The all or nothing mentality isn't going to work.

Another thing that I'm going to say is to shift your mindset. Start telling yourself that you are healthy, happy, and whole. Tell yourself, you lose weight easily and effortlessly, you've already lost weight and feel great in your body. I have my women look in the mirror and say I love you, I honor you, I am you, and I accept you. It's these simple things that make a really big difference.

When we want to make something a lifestyle, it starts with small changes. Tony Robbins always said, "All we want to know is that we progressed forward. You don't need to win a gold medal tomorrow. You just need to take a step on your way there."

What I want to encourage you to do in that exercise is to write down what defines you, who is the woman that you are. Who is Sadie? Who do you want that to be? From there, start living into her more and more. Read that embodiment of you when you wake up in the morning and when you go to bed at night.

Put in there she's somebody who enjoys a healthy and fit lifestyle. It's a part of who she is. Start identifying as somebody that's healthy and fit instead of as somebody that is a dieter who always struggled with her weight. Don't identify as somebody who doesn't see how she's ever going to get here because of all the negativity.

FEEDING YOUR SUBCONSCIOUS MIND

Dave: Melissa, can I jump in there? I've got a question for you about what you're saying. There are so many words of wisdom in there. One thing you said is to write down who is Sadie and this could be for anyone reading this book. Then you mentioned writing it down and looking at it in the morning and the evening. Is that step in itself good enough? Will that make any difference?

Melissa: Yes, yeah. Any time you can feed yourself something, you're feeding your subconscious mind. You want to feed it the highest, most potent information possible.

Turn off your TVs, guys, stop watching reality shows and people yelling at each other or the news before you go to sleep. Give yourself something to digest that will be on repeat in your subconscious mind.

I'm a hypnotherapist as well, and I'll do weight-loss hypnosis and different things for my clients. It's that subconscious re-patterning that really helps us. You don't even need hypnosis.

What I'm saying is you just want to start feeding yourself. Say to yourself you're fit and healthy, you're fit and healthy, you're fit and healthy. Repeat it over and over. I lose weight with ease, over and over as you fall asleep at night.

Reading who you are is going to cement it in your mind when waking up. When you're sleeping, you go into a hypnotic state. When you wake up, you're still in a hypnotic state, so you're highly prone to taking that in. It's going to penetrate your subconscious before your conscious mind can come in to take over with its negativity. With its banter and repeated tapes that are on repeat from days before.

We have 80,000 thoughts that are on repeat daily, many of which are from the preceding 72 hours. Before you let those come in, let's hit your mind with something really beautiful. Your subconscious mind doesn't know the difference between a dream and reality, so start feeding it what you want and start in the morning.

Dave: Melissa, this is so awesome, and I just want to give you a little anecdote. I've done this myself fairly recently. I read this book called *The Purpose Driven Life*, and at the end, the last chapter is all about developing this purpose statement. I created my purpose statement, and I have it on my desktop, on my computer. In the morning and the night, I read it and recite that back to myself.

That's it; that's all I do with it. It has changed my daily actions every single day since I've written it out and I think that's exactly what you're saying. Sadie, and everyone else reading, if you start to look at your life and look at yourself through a different lens, you will become that different version of yourself you're hoping to become.

Melissa: Hands down. I love that you just said that, yes.

WHAT YOU GAIN VERSUS WHAT YOU GIVE UP

Dave: Now, for Sadie, I think that's awesome advice. You gave another statement that I want to go back to because it sounded so powerful. You said, shift into what you're gaining, not what you're giving up. What does that mean for Sadie and everyone else?

Melissa: Because people have this notion around being healthy as if it's this huge sacrifice. Like you have to walk around eating cardboard and grilled chicken and broccoli.

Dave: And cotton balls dipped in orange juice.

Melissa: Yes, and cotton balls dipped in orange juice, didn't you know? Don't you love my words of wisdom? Anyway, okay, I'm deviating. This is my ADD mind going wild.

Dave: Shift into what you're gaining, not what you're giving up. What does that look like?

Melissa: I appreciate that, Dave. Okay, it's looking at what are you going to gain from being your best self.

What is it going to feel like to achieve this goal for yourself? What is it going to be for you? How is this going to benefit you? How good does it feel to wake up and drink warm water with lemon instead of either having coffee right away or starving yourself until noon?

How good is it going to feel to read a statement about yourself that's beautiful instead of waking up to negative banter and running out the door attracting more of what you don't want? How good is it going to feel to move your body and connect? Look at all the benefits. What are you gaining? I always tell people, fitness is a happiness pill. It is like breathing. It is, I believe, aside from breathing, the best thing you could do for yourself for happiness. For sleep, to de-stress.

There is absolutely nothing—when you break it down—you're giving up, but you have to shift into this. When you get out of the dieter's mindset, you recognize you can have whatever foods you want, whenever you want them.

You'll find that the foods you think you'd want to go crazy on if given the opportunity no longer are what you desire because they don't feel good. That will happen in time, but you just want to start off looking at what you're getting instead of what you're giving up. Once you shift your mindset, that's all you need for success. That's it.

Dave: I love that example you gave. One of the things you just eluded to was the fact your tastes for certain foods will actually change.

I can imagine someone like Sadie who's saying, "Yeah, I'm never going to want to be a healthy eater just naturally." What you're saying is as you progressively take these baby steps toward cleaning up your diet, your tastes are going to change. So your desires for unhealthy food are declining and eventually go away completely. Is that what your message is saying?

Melissa: Hands down. Even in my journey, I didn't all of a sudden say, "Ah, I want to clean eat." No, it was in steps. Then I started going, "Wow, I just feel so good doing this. Okay, it's fun cooking this way, and I like knowing what's in my body and this is great." Again it's living in the rainbow, not in the black and white.

Sadie, you don't need to wake up tomorrow and green juice every day and no longer eat carbs and give up chocolate. It doesn't have to be that way at all. In fact, it's good to have balance. It's good to have what you want when you want it. That's what being healthy is. It does happen in baby steps.

I have a client who signed up with me and said, "You will never get me to stop drinking soda, I love it." I said, "Okay, that's fine with me. Let's get started."

Dave: She was probably shocked.

Melissa: I don't forbid anything. That's not why you're working with me. That isn't what this is about. Then about three weeks in she says, "Yeah, it's interesting, I noticed I'm only having a few sodas a week now, I'm down to three." I was like, "Oh, okay, that's good, so do you feel good?" She says, "Yeah, it's weird, I don't even really want them." Then, all of a sudden, she's telling me she's down to one, and she says, "Most of them, they're like sugar syrup." I said, "Yeah, yeah."

Again, I hardly said anything. She's down to one, and she ended up beautifully getting pregnant, which was something she wanted with her husband. It just happened so quickly. Then she says, "Now that's the last thing I want to give my child."

She's six months into her pregnancy, and she says, "I can't believe I used to drink soda, it makes me sick even thinking about it." She was addicted to soda for a decade. It was such a quick shift.

When it's on your terms, and you don't feel somebody's forcing you to do something, you start getting in alignment. You're like, "Oh, this is interesting." You want to make choices that serve you; you just do.

Dave: What a neat story because I'm sure if you ask that client when you first started working with her, "Can you imagine your life when it's soda-free?" And she probably would have said, "Oh, there's no way I'm cutting out my soda." And then all of a sudden…

Melissa: That was her contingency to work with me. She was like, "You can't get me off soda." I was like, "That's fine."

Dave: Low and behold, however many months later, she's living a lifestyle that is soda-free. Even though she said, that would absolutely never happen.

Melissa: Not only that, she's calling it sugar syrup. I was hysterically laughing. She's like, "I don't know what you're doing to me." I was like, "I know, so awful! All these things I'm having you do."

She's so proud of herself, and it all just happened in a way that just felt good. But I didn't sit there and say, "No soda!" because what will that do?

Her subconscious mind is going to be saying, "Soda, soda, soda, soda." Then she'll want it more than ever, just like we do. We're like little kids. You tell us we can't have something even if we're saying to ourselves that we can. So what do we do? We go and eat it until it's all gone.

SMALL CHANGES REALLY DO ADD UP

Dave: That's an interesting point, too. So, if Sadie was to say, "Okay, I want to have a healthy lifestyle, and that means not eating any sugar. So I'm not going to eat sugar."

It's this self-induced rule. That rule probably won't last very long because it's like you said, that's living in the black and white as opposed to the rainbow in between. What would be a better approach for someone who's trying to shift their mindset, without just going black and white?

Melissa: Meet yourself where you're at. If you're not working out right now, you're not going to go and work out seven days this week. You might for one week and then what's going to happen?

You're not going to do it, and then you're going to tell yourself you're a failure. You're going to compare yourself to the one week when you made it for seven days. How about you just start off with two days? 30 minutes for two days, and do that for two weeks. Then, add in a third day.

If you're eating out every meal, how about you just start saying, "You know what? This week I'm going to pick one meal, and I'm going to bring my breakfast each day." Or if you're not eating breakfast, how about you just start having breakfast.

It doesn't have to be these big things. It's amazing how just one small change will change it all for you. You will feel so much better and all of a sudden you feel more proud of yourself. Then you think, "I think I could do that for another meal." And then you end up making more positive changes.

Dave: What a difference that would be. Say you decided that you're going to exercise once this week as opposed to seven times this week. You did that and then chose to throw in a bonus workout. You just worked out twice this week. What a difference in mental reward or mindset you'd be in after superseding your goal, going far past it. As opposed to, like you said, "Okay, I'll go seven days per week. I didn't do it again. I'm a failure. I suck. I can't do this." What a difference.

Melissa: Huge, right.

Dave: Now, Melissa, I feel like we can keep talking for a long time, but we do need to finish up. Now, you have offered up a free, really cool program, and it's called Conquer Your Cravings. This is free for everyone who's reading this book. Can you tell us quickly, what that's all about?

HOW TO CONQUER YOUR CRAVINGS

Melissa: Yeah, this is awesome. I love this thing so much. I'm really big on helping people recognize how their emotions play a big role in the foods that they're choosing, what they're triggered by, and how the way they eat often results in self-sabotage and making them feel bad. Like you took 10 steps back in your diet.

This program is a class you can listen to. There are handouts and a refrigerator magnet that goes along with it.

Like I told you, I'm huge on the psychological, behavioral patterns we have around food and interrupting those, while having that happen in a way through awareness and implementing these steps.

Doing this will help you lose weight effortlessly and also understand your cravings so you can conquer them. It breaks them down into two categories—head and heart cravings. Each of those has a different set of foods and action steps. Most likely, you'll identify with both of them; however, one will be more dominant.

It's super helpful. People love it. People are just obsessed with it and told me it has changed their lives; it's opened them up. So I'm just really excited and wanted to make sure your readers had access to this as well.

Dave: Awesome, I appreciate it. And for all the readers, you can get a direct link to the Conquer Your Cravings Kit in the *Resources* section at the end of this chapter.

Melissa, thanks again for joining us today and just for the practical wisdom. But I really appreciate you looking at this psychological side. I think you've identified very well with the cause of where Sadie's question is coming from, this disbelief that she can do it. Thanks for really tapping into that and giving us so many actionable steps that we can use.

Melissa: Oh, my god, of course. Sadie, good luck, and girl, feel free to reach out for anything you need. I've totally been there, and I get it. And everybody reading, thank you so much for your time. I hope this spoke to you today.

Dave: Yeah, and for Sadie and anyone else who wants to be in touch with Melissa, I'll put a link to her website in the *Resources* section, and you can contact her there. I know she'll be happy to help out. Thanks again, Melissa.

Melissa: All right, thanks so much, Dave. Thank you for having me.

RESOURCES

Melissa's Website: http://melissakathryn.com

Conquer Your Cravings Kit:
http://makeyourbodywork.com/mk-cravings

CHAPTER 2:

WHY IS IT EASIER FOR EVERYONE ELSE?

From the interview in chapter 1, you know that your mindset will determine your success. What you believe about yourself will fuel your subconscious mind, and those beliefs will manifest into reality.

This "law of attraction," where your positive mindset leads to positive outcomes in your life, likely won't happen all at once. But, over time your new mindset and lifestyle *will* produce the body you're looking for.

This is true for you. Still, it can sometimes seem like it's happening so much easier for everyone else. It's as if everyone has their lives all put together, while your changes are taking forever.

That's certainly how Corina felt:

> *"I have always been the fat one. In my family, growing up at school, with my friends now as an adult. I have always felt like I'm fighting an unfair battle, one that seems easy for others.*
>
> *While I know that's not entirely true, it is how I feel. I've tried and failed at changing my weight in the past, and it's hard to start again when I know that the results might be the same. I'm not really sure what I'm looking for, maybe just some motivation to try again? I don't like my body and I want to change it. Help me?"*

These feelings of being "the fat one" are descriptive for so many people. But these are lies that can be quieted and replaced with a positive message that will lead to change.

MEET DAI MANUEL

Dai Manuel is a Certified Lifestyle Mentor and Executive Performance Coach. He's an author, motivational speaker, and educator who speaks the truth about healthy living and how people can release weight.

His goal is to inspire people around the world to take charge of their life and health. He did himself, as an overweight teenager who was dealing with thoughts of suicide, so he knows it's possible for anyone who is committed to making change.

THE INTERVIEW

Dave: Hey, Dai, thanks so much for joining me in this interview today.

Dai: Hey, thank you, Dave, I'm excited for the opportunity, this is really, really cool. Thanks.

Dave: A quick little background for the readers is you and I we were at a conference just recently here in Vancouver actually, it's called the CanFit, it's a fitness conference, and I caught one of your sessions. You and I had never crossed paths before, and thought, oh, this guy, you're full of energy. You just had a great presence about you, and I knew I wanted to hear your story.

Dai: (laughs) Well, I appreciate that, I always try to bring it. When I present especially I am a bit of a high-energy guy, a lot of squirrel moments, but that's just who I am. Thank you.

Dave: No, it's awesome. Then, actually, I was checking you out online and just seeing your whole story and you have a really neat story, like a personal story about how you got all wrapped up in the fitness industry and I was wondering if you could start off by telling the readers what that was all about.

IT WASN'T ALWAYS EASY: DAI, THE OVERWEIGHT TEENAGER

Dai: Yeah, sure, Dave. Thanks. A lot of people in the fitness industry, they come from sport, right? They played sport, typically, to a fairly high level or they just have a real passion for fitness and moving their body and I didn't come from that, okay? In fact, from about the age of nine, ten years old I started to put weight on, I did that all on my own volition, I did the usual.

I ate unhealthy foods, quite a bit of 'em, and I didn't move my body very much, I played a lot of video games. Over time, by age 14, I was quite overweight and I didn't like that anymore.

I hit a certain point where I was like, I want more in life and I'm gonna date myself right now. I didn't have the luxury of Google back then. When I decided I wanted to get a little healthier I went to a library, I got books out, I reached out to people I felt knew what they were doing.

And, fortunately for me, my parents were very supportive of me wanting to make that transformation, and bought me a mountain bike. My dad, I remember him taking me to pick it up, it was amazing.

I got out on my mountain bike, I'd start riding couple hours every day, I started educating myself about nutrition, and just making smarter choices, but doing that every single day. It's one thing to choose to make some significant changes, but when you actually apply action to those choices, that's where we really start to see good things start to happen.

You know how it goes, that first step's always the hardest step, but once you start making some steps and you start to get more comfortable with that feeling that you start to create in yourself, and you start to gain that confidence, the education then takes over and you do intrinsically know what to do.

Fortunately for me, after about 20 months I lost the weight, kick-started my puberty finally, that also helped because I started to put on some muscle mass, I started to grow, I then got into weight training and I just had a real passion for helping others do the same thing.

That was really the catalyst that got me interested in health and fitness, especially transformations, and fast forward, I've been doing it now for well over 20 years, earning an income in the fitness industry.

I like to qualify that because I know a lot of people who treat it more like a hobby, which there is nothing wrong with that, but I actually support my family doing this and it's been a lot of fun. I've worked in a lot of different capacities in the industry and I just love it. I love it. And meeting you at Canfitpro, it's just another reason why I love that tribe, these health professionals, because we're all on a similar mission. We're looking to change people and to really help them live their life to the fullest.

Dave: I appreciate you saying you didn't come from a background of sport because, you're right, a lot of us fitness professionals do have that sports background. I'm on your website right now and I'm taking a look, you have a great before and after picture and you as a teenager, to be honest, you don't look anything like you look right now. When I met you I thought, this guy, he must've played football or rugby 'cause you're a big, muscular guy, but just like you said, your story is not that at all.

Dai: Yeah, I am fortunate from a genetic standpoint that if I want to put weight on whether it's fat or muscle, I can do it pretty easily. So as soon as I started applying some basic nutritional principles, feeding my body what it wanted, and what it needed to fuel me well, then I started to move weight or start moving under load, I really just started to accelerate at that.

And it opened my eyes to a lot of other things. I got into martial arts, I started hiking and rock climbing. Then eventually, in 2007, I got into CrossFit and that's really been my passion ever since, the last 10 years I've been doing that at different levels and competing at it and I really do enjoy that a lot.

RECONNECT TO "THAT FEELING"

Dave: It's really cool hearing your story because I think actually you can probably relate a fair bit to Karina's question that we're talking about today where she talks about always feeling a little bit on the outside and feeling like it looks so easy for everyone else but for her she's just not happy with her own fitness, her own body.

30

When you were reading her question, what kind of thoughts went through your head?

Dai: Well, Dave, you and I both know this very well because we work with a lot of different types of people, all walks of life, all shapes, all sizes, all abilities, as trainers, health professionals, personal trainers, whatever.

I always talk about the muscle I've got to work with first is that muscle between the ears. That's the one that tends to be the one that's least developed in a lot of folks, especially when they're starting to think about getting a little healthier, getting a little fitter.

When I read Karina's question, I remember back to my own transformations and I was intimidated. I think we all are because we get lost. We start to go down that rabbit hole of seeking out information to educate ourselves on how to actually make that change happen, before we've started to look internally at why do we want to make those changes happen.

I want to qualify that a little bit, when I say why, and during my presentation I alluded to this a little bit as far as how trainers communicate their message online or offline, and it's that emotional connection we have with the choices we make everyday. What is it intrinsically that motivates us to choose to get up in the morning, because it's hard. When you're out of shape or as I say, in that state of unhealth, everything is difficult.

I always equate it back to remember that last time you had the flu and I'm talking not just a "man flu," but a full on flu. You want nothing but sitting on the couch, putting on Netflix, and you just want nothing to do with the world because you're sick and you feel like garbage. It's really hard to motivate yourself to move when you're in that state.

You can imagine, if you've got someone with a chronic ailment, then that compounds that situation because you're like that everyday. When you've been in that state for a long amount of time, you don't remember what it's like to feel good. You don't know what it feels like to be healthy and to be able to wake up with that hop, skip, and a jump being excited for the day ahead of you. Getting reconnected to that feeling is really, really important.

DAI'S MOTIVATION. WHAT'S YOURS?

Dave: When you were going through your transformation as a young teenager, do you remember that? You talked about your dad giving you a mountain bike, and to be honest, I know you're just sort of glossing over your story, and you said, "I started making healthier eating choices." Were there points where you thought, "This isn't worth it," or "I don't want to do this," or "I just want to go get a McDonald's happy meal?"

Dai: Yeah, yeah. Well, for me, I was thinking long-term. And listen, let's be honest, I was 14-years-old, I'm prepubescent at that time because I hadn't really started puberty, but I saw the other kids in school, especially the other grade eights, grade nines, and they had girlfriends, girls took them seriously. I was motivated to get a girlfriend. And to me, it was like, I've got to get healthy, I've got to be fit, I gotta change how I am now, at least externally.

It wasn't until many years later that I really had to deal with the internal side of things. What I mean by that is there was some other emotional stuff I had to work through much later on in life, in my 20s I started to work through that and even into my 30s I was working on some stuff. Working on ourselves psychologically, emotionally, it's an ongoing process.

The physical piece, though, if we're really talking about the physical transformation, it's intimidating. I remember going to the gym for the first time. I was mountain biking everyday, I had been consistent with that for about four months, I had lost a bunch of weight, but now I wanted to start gaining some muscle mass, I wanted to start to fill out.

I remember going to the gym and I was scared man, because I had no idea what the hell this place is, there was all this steel, there were these machines these people were running on, there were these little exercise bikes. They had classes, you know, the step classes were big back then, it was late 80s, early 90s, you can imagine. StairMasters all over the place, Jane Fonda was it. That was it. Now people are probably wondering, "How old is this dude?"

How to Overcome Discouragement

I was intimated and it's a scary place to go because you just don't know. You don't know what to do, you don't know how you're gonna do it, and you do have that little bit of a connection with the why, you want to make the change, you know it's important to make the change, but when you don't have a community to plug into or to that supportive network to help you it can be really problematic. And when I say problematic, it will eventually lead to that point where you say, "Is this really worth it? I'm too scared, I'm fearful, I don't think I can do this right now."

The community piece, and that's where I was going with that question, was there was days, I want to answer your question, there were days where I would get very discouraged, things weren't happening fast enough, because I wanted it to happen right now. It took 20 months for me to really lose all the weight and to change to the point where I felt more confident in my physicality and my ability.

But there were times, especially after six, seven months, I was like, man, I would much rather just crush a pizza with a buddy, play some video games, and not work out. Just not do that thing that I know I really want to be doing, and I think that's the difference, right? Because a lot of us have that internal dialogue, "Oh, I really should do this." "If I had this I would do that." "Is it really worth it?"

There has to be that shift where it really becomes a lifestyle decision, it becomes sustainable because it's automatic. You're not really thinking about it anymore. It's like, "I want to do this." Why? Because, 5, 10, 20 years from now I'm hopeful that my kids have their own kids so they can experience what I've been experiencing with them right now, but so I can be that active granddad with them, right? Or I can travel the world and I can see some sights, go see some amazing places and experience some cultures, but do it firsthand.

Actually go and walk around and touch things and connect with people and not be limited on my physicality because I've put some daily action in place today, tomorrow, for weeks, and months, and years to come that's going to best set me up for that ideal future that I have pictured in my mind. So that's that sort of external motivator even though I'm visualizing it internally.

Dave: I love it. There's a couple key things that I want to point out that you said there. When you talked about going to the gym and it being that scary moment,

Karina in her question she says, "I'm fighting an unfair battle, one that seems easy for others." And so I love that you talked about it was hard, it was scary, it was uncomfortable, and as you were talking, Dai, man, that's the exact same story for me.

I remember going to the gym the first time and I sat on a machine bench press and realized I could put basically no weight on and was so embarrassed, so I walked on the treadmill, jogged for like 10 minutes, and then left and was like I'm never going back there again.

Probably the same motivation as you, I probably wanted to impress a girl so I went back to the gym. But to Karina's point where she says it's an unfair battle, that's you and I, we're both in the fitness industry and we felt that way. And I know and I'm sure you would say the same thing working with thousands of clients, every single person feels that way.

YOU ARE WRITING YOUR OWN STORY

Dai: I really do believe that, to some extent, just some are better at masking it. I appreciate Karina being open and transparent and honest with how she's feeling. If you tell yourself that story, so if I'm speaking directly to her right now, she's reading, if you continue to tell yourself that story, you are writing your story. You can change that. You are going to feel uncomfortable, okay, I'm not going to deny it. It's not going to be fun, fun fun.

I mean, I hope it gets to the point where you're like, "This is fun, I like doing this, I really want to do it, I want to go to the gym everyday or I want to go for that hike with my friends, I want to go to the pool and go for a swim," whatever. But there's going to have to be a point where you have to write a story for yourself and really tie an emotional connection to that why that motivates you.

Once you have that emotional connection, it's different, right? We can talk about the "how's" and the "what's" all day long. You and I can talk about, "Oh, this is how you do a proper squat, this is how you do a proper push-up, here's a great way where to position your hands on the bench press machine," we can have those conversations, but that's really just the how and the what.

But for us to tell people, well, here's why you should do this, unless they're emotionally vested in that, it's a hard sell and it's not necessarily a sustainable sell. That's why you see a lot of it happen, look at what we're coming up to, it's going to be New Years soon. The gyms are flocked with people, but by anywhere from the third week to mid-February, it's more than half are gone. It's a scary place.

I hate that aspect because there was something, somewhere that made them decide that, "I'm going to set myself a resolution to be healthier this year." And I believe that that's truly what they want, but they may be unsure about how they're going to sustain that.

And really, why are they making that decision? Because they think it's a good idea, or is it because maybe they have a health condition that they really need to deal with? Well, if that's the case, then when life and death comes into it, we make decisions pretty quickly. A lot of time these health issues that sneak up on us, they do, they take years to manifest themselves and by that point, when they do, we're always like, oh my gosh, now what am I gonna do, and it takes a long time to get back.

ADOPTING THE LONG-TERM MINDSET

Dave: You know another thing that I really like that you emphasize, a couple times you mentioned that your weight-loss journey was a 20-month journey. Twenty months. Two years of pushing forward toward this goal that maybe at some point seemed out of reach. How did you get yourself into a mindset where you thought long-term? Because you even said that. You said you were in this for the long-term, which blows my mind that you're a 14-year-old boy thinking long-term. How do you get that mindset?

Dai: Well, I wasn't happy with myself. I wasn't diagnosed as being depressed, but I definitely withdrew at times. And you know what was really a telltale sign, I think, was the fact, I remember when a number of years ago we decided to be more vocal, based on what, I was in the equipment industry. Selling specialized fitness equipment, accessories, supplements, all that kind of stuff. We decided that we were going to be a bit more vocal about my background and how I got started. I wasn't sharing this publicly back then.

I remember asking my mom to find some photos of me as a kid, especially when I was overweight. It was hard to find any photos, and it's not for lack of my parents trying to take photos, it's just I did shy away from photos. I remember purposefully trying to duck out of photos because I didn't want anything, I didn't want to be seen. To get over that it just took a decision to do it and to continue to do it.

Now I joke with people, you know what's even more powerful than just doing it, being able to say you just did it. When you get to that point, you're talking about actually accomplishing it and speaking in that kind of a language is very powerful from a psychological standpoint, as well. I always tell people, even some of my clients that I work with, I'm like, "Just send me a text with 'just did it,' #justdidit." That's all I need.

That's your little bit of accountability, just tell me when it's been done. Don't tell me you're going to go to the gym, don't tell me you're going to do this, you're going to do that, you're going to eat better, no, just tell me when you've done it. That is pretty cool. But you've got to also be accountable to yourself, right?

Dave: You know, that idea of "just did it" is so powerful. Sometimes when I send out e-mails, I'll send out research or just new articles I've written, usually about weight-loss, to my mailing list. I'll get people that we've never met before and they'll send me back, sometimes it's just a one-liner, I got one yesterday. This girl wrote back and she said, "I lost 2 kgs this week." And that's all she said in the e-mail, didn't even sign it with her name or anything, but I just thought, there is that pride of "Hey, I used to be stuck and now I just did it."

Dai: I love it, man. That is so cool. It's great, right? And it's why we do what we do. It's those little victories, man. I love celebrating every single one of them with anybody who reaches out to me. It's like, "Yeah, I'll give you a virtual high-five on that one, keep going!" Because, again, it's creating that community and I really do feel that community's what keeps us engaged and helps us on the days where we're feeling low.

There's times where we have to, we need someone to psychologically pick us back up, dust us off, and tell us it's going to be okay. And it's all right to draw a line in the sand and step over because it's a new day.

Dave: And that's a great message again. In Karina's message she talks about how she's failed in the past and just doesn't feel that she can start again. Actually, her question she says, "Maybe I just need some motivation to try again."

Dai: Yeah. Well stated. I never like to be the bad cop, but there comes a point where you just got to say, "Okay, yeah, I screwed up, I tripped, I made some mistakes, whatever. It already happened, I can't dwell on that anymore."

I don't want to hear about it. Done. I acknowledge it, you said it, moving on. All right, so let's figure out how to get to the next part. How do we overcome this, get you back to what you know you want to be doing? I know you want to do this, I know you want to feel better, so what do we need to do to make that happen?

Dave: You talked a lot about "finding your why" and it sounds like you found your why and that's something that's carried through and now you really enjoy it. I like that piece you said, "Eventually it won't be so hard and you're just going to enjoy doing this stuff." How do you walk someone through finding their why when they don't know what their why is?

FINDING YOUR REASON "WHY?"

Dai: There are some great resources. Tony Robbins, obviously, is a big why guy. He's self-proclaimed "why guy." You can check out some of his TED Talks, he talks about this, especially that intrinsic connection with our why's and how we discover those. Simon Sineck is someone that's very well-known for that, as well, and he's got a book called "Start With Why," and I love his TED Talk, as well, it's about a 20-minute TED Talk. It's one of the top three or four TED Talks most viewed. Those are ones I would highly encourage people to check them out, and if you want more, then go to their websites or get their books.

It talks about this process. It's a marathon, it's not a sprint. It's not something that you can just make up or invent over night, it has to be a process that you live through and you really have to be introspective in that process, but it's really finding out what are you passionate about. I don't like to limit people to one passion. There are multiple passions in people's lives and I'm really big on family, I'm big on entrepreneurship, I'm also big on helping people.

So with me, I've got these three passions and I was always like, "Well, how do I fuel all three of those?" This is me being selfish, too, right? When I help people, I'm doing it to help them, but trust me, I get a lot of value from that, it makes me very happy. Does that make me a bad guy? No, but I'm very much in tune with that and it's what motivates me to continue doing it, because I really love it.

Not necessarily everybody's careers are going to be in an area they feel that passionate about. But we have lots of time outside of our careers to do things that we are passionate about. What are those things that drive you? Maybe it does get to a point where you're like, "You know what? I really want to be doing more of what I love."

I left my job, my career of 17 years to do what I'm doing now full-time. It got to a point and I left a great career. I got a lot of friends that they're like, "What the hell are you doing, are you crazy?" We gave away all of our stuff, we literally packed what we could into our SUV and we've been on the road just over a year now.

Me, my family, we're homeschooling our kids, it's quite the transition, you know, going from a traditional 17-year career in business to now doing what I'm doing, which is talking to cool people like you and your communities and really just helping people live lives of awesomeness. That's really what I'm trying to do, but it's a night and day difference.

Was I uncomfortable going through that process? Am I still uncomfortable? Hell yeah. There are days I wake up I'm like, man, maybe I should get a job. I got some bills. There's a lot of fear, but you know what, and this is the one thing, Dave, anybody who's reading:

Ask yourself, 10 years from now, if you were to look back on some of these hard decisions and you saw that you had gone the easy direction just because you wanted to play it safe, rather than really risking it and trying for something that you knew you really, really wanted, how are you going to feel about that situation?

Are you going to feel regretful? Are you going to be kicking yourself saying, "Man, I really wish I gave that a go?"

For me, I could not answer that question. I couldn't answer it honestly at least without realising that I would be kicking myself if I didn't take a risk. I know I'll be sad, 'cause I'd rather try it and fail at it but then I can look back and say, "Man, I tried and it was awesome, I learned a lot from it," but, you know, so what is the worst that can happen, right? What is the worst that can happen?

You get up January 1st, you decide to go to the gym, you go get a workout in, you sweat a little bit, you get a little intimidated, sure, but maybe you meet a couple cool friends. There's so many other possibilities. You can write so many different stories. But what's really the worst that's going to happen?

Dave: And to be patient with that. Because when you're telling your story about leaving your career and jumping into full-time entrepreneurship I'm sure it wasn't that first day or that first week that you were like, "Yes, I've made it, I'm a success." It takes time. Same for Karina. If you get up and say, "Hey, today I'm going to go back to the gym," you might not make those friends, you might feel awful, it might be intimidating, you might think, "I never want to go back," but four weeks from now or two months from now, that will change.

Dai: Absolutely and I really believe it. I'm not saying there won't be days where things aren't going your way. That's life, that's what makes it interesting. If it was groundhog's day everyday, it would be too predictable, We'd all be a bunch of lemmings. That's just not how it works. Being okay with the unpredictability of life, that's what makes it interesting. Just be okay with the process and trust in the process. I think that is the biggest thing because sometimes we are very much in a "now economy" and we are used to getting information faster than we have ever been able to before.

But still when it comes to our fitness and our health, I see so many people buying into the newest fad, the newest hack, and I'm like, "Just get back to basics, find something that you can do in your already busy lifestyle." Don't try to reinvent your lifestyle to accommodate some new program versus find something that overlays with what you're already doing because that makes it sustainable for the rest of your life because it's part of your life. It's this whole process. Trust that good things will happen if you start making good decisions every day.

Dave: Awesome. I love the positivity of that message and it's true, it is true.

Dai: Yeah, just start. Pay yourself first. I'll qualify that really quickly. What I mean by that is, carve out minimum 30 minutes a day for you. And be selfish. This is your time. Nobody else can infringe on this. It is, this block of time, above and beyond anything else that's on your plate, has to happen. It's unconditional.

You matter. You are important. To be the best version of yourself, to be the best parent, the best friend, the best guardian, the best coworker, you need to have your body, mind, and spirit in alignment. You need to be healthy, you need to be feeling good.

What can you do with 2% of your 24 hours that is going to invest in your body, mind, and spirit? Maybe that's moving a little bit with purpose, practicing meditation, doing some personal development, whatever it might be, make a 30-minute commitment to yourself every day.

Like flossing your teeth. It's something that's gotta happen. Every day. If you can carve out that time, good things will happen. It might grow. There might be days you give yourself an hour, but no matter what, 2% of every 24 hours is invested in you.

Dave: I love that and I love the fact that you gave some examples of it doesn't have to be exercise because I know we talked a lot about exercise today, but there are many different ways you can invest in yourself.

Dai: It's like, if you give me 30 minutes I'm going to change your life, but that's the starter point, right? I'm not saying that's the end-all be-all. Is that all you have to do? Well, no, but it's the minimum you have to do.

RESOURCES

Dai's Website: https://www.daimanuel.com/

Tony Robbin's Why TED Talk: http://makeyourbodywork.com/tony-robbins-why

Simon Sinek's TED Talk: http://makeyourbodywork.com/simon-sinek-why

CHAPTER 3:

WHAT'S GETTING IN YOUR WAY?

I hope that my interview with Dai Manuel in the last chapter reinforced that you are not alone when it comes to wanting change, but feeling like it's a bit out of reach. Even people who seemingly have it all together still struggle with aspects of their appearance and who they are. Nobody is perfectly satisfied. We all want change.

That's why you're reading this book. You want change. You want to win your battle against weight loss, even if it takes some time, effort, and energy.

But just how much are you willing to sacrifice to get there? How much *should* you sacrifice?

If losing a few pounds requires a complete overhaul of your life – spending hours in the gym, preparing organic meals from scratch, and going to bed by 9 pm – is it really worth it?

There are other priorities in life besides staying healthy and fit. How can you make enough changes to your life to see results without giving up everything else?

Gurdeep alluded to this very question. For her, it was her job that was getting in the way:

> "Dave, I work as a marketing executive. I love my work and I believe in the products we sell but I probably sit 80% of my day and even though I exercise and eat well, I work for a health food company dammit, I am still gaining weight and feeling my age. Part of me would like to give it all up and focus on getting my health back on track, but that's not in the cards right now. My question is about other things we business people can do to stay in peak shape, aside from just going to the gym and trying to say no to snacks that make their way into our office. I need to follow a plan. I'll check the boxes if I know which ones I should be checking. Thanks for any ideas."

Gurdeep struggled with her work-life balance, but for you, it might be something different. You only have so much time in the day, and prioritizing some of that time for your health isn't going to be easy.

Whether it's work, family life, social commitments, or anything else that demands your time, at some point you have to say, "It's time to focus on me."

MEET IREENE SINIAKIS

Ireene Siniakis is a health coach who has worked in the health and wellness industry for over 25 years. Her extensive training in food and life coaching, as well as her personal trainer and fitness coaching certifications, have made her a wellness authority.

She has worked as a Corporate Health Consultant and authored the book "The Healthy Executive."

THE INTERVIEW

Dave: Hey Ireene, thanks so much for joining me in this interview today.

Ireene: Hey Dave, how are you doing?

Dave: Good, good. Thanks for being here. I'm excited to have you. Before we dive into the question for today, I was looking on your website, and I saw a line you wrote. It's about what you do and who you work with, and you said, "I get great satisfaction out of coaching busy professionals to get back into shape." I was wondering if you could tell us why. Why do you like working with busy professionals?

Ireene: Thanks, Dave. Again, thanks for having me. I love working with busy professionals because I actually understand them. I was that person too, and I understand there's a lot of people in offices working the grind. They do eight, nine, ten hours.

They're sitting on their butts all day, and they're committed to their job. They neglect themselves because they're so committed to their job or their careers. They just kind of lose sight of their health and themselves, because they're on this hamster wheel.

I love it because I help them pull it all back in and realize that unless they put themselves first, their health and wellbeing are limited, they're just going to continue on this hamster wheel. I love to work with busy people because I actually understand what they're going through. I used to work in that corporate, "Go, go, go," type of environment.

Over a period of time, we all tend to get that extra weight hanging around our waistline and our hips. As a woman I can say, it constantly pulls on your mind and gets you down and out. I hear from people—especially women—all the time they don't want to go to certain functions because they don't know what to wear. And then there's a domino effect. I love to work with those particular people because I truly understand what they're going through.

Dave: I'd like to ask you a little bit more about your own personal story. Can you talk about your career arch? Like what were you doing in the business world before, and how did you decide at some point that you were going to make the shift into the health world?

IREENE'S PERSONAL STORY

Ireene: I was working in the corporate environment and in a sales job through my twenties and thirties. I never really felt fulfilled. I liked my job, and I liked the people that I worked with, but something was always was missing. I remember a friend of mine, a professional sportsman, said to me, "Do what you like but make it your job." I thought, "What do I like?" I thought, "Well, I like going to the gym."

I was a personal trainer, and I had my private clients on the side after work. I always had one or two clients. But then I thought, "What do I like?" I thought, "Well yeah, I like going to the gym and helping people."

I had my PT clients, and I thought, "Now I need to work in the industry full-time," so I went to work for a magazine, *Women's Health and Fitness*. I did that for three years, and then I worked for a golfing publication. It was always something in the sport and health industry. But something was still missing even while I was doing my personal training.

I was working on health and wellbeing, but I felt like people weren't really getting the results that they were wanting to get. I thought, "It's the food, 80% it's the food," so I became a food coach and then I could coach my clients in food and nutrition.

Years past by, and I thought, "Well, something's still not right. Something's still missing. Why are some of these people still not getting results while some are, and what makes the difference?"

In my early thirties, I hurt my back. I actually did it in my sleep. I felt like my back just gave way, and I had to have surgery instantly because my leg went numb. When I was going through that for two to three months, I was lying on my back thinking, "Oh God, I just want to be normal again. I just want to feel good." I thought that I would never ever neglect my health ever again.

After sitting at a desk all day, I was going to the gym and training the body parts that I liked: my legs or my arms. But I was always neglecting my abs or my core. I had a really weak core, and like I said, I hurt my back. I got slapped in the face from the universe, and it said, "Hey wake up yourself. It's time for you to take control."

That prompted me to work full-time in fitness. Over the last eight years, I've worked in corporate health and wellbeing, managing a large corporate client that has thousands of employees. I have a team of trainers who work for me, and we deliver health and wellbeing programs.

I actually love helping people but what I really love the most is helping people who actually want results. I help these people get from A to B. They are committed, and they really want it. They've suffered long enough.

It's great. That's kind of my story. I've lived it, I've seen it. I've had something happen to me that was traumatic at the time. I've made that shift, and I really encourage people by saying, "Don't wait until something bad happens. Without your health, you're limited."

With the community being 60-70% overweight, it's really time that we wake up and take our health more seriously and do something about it because it's getting worse. What they're putting in our foods is getting worse. We're just really like, "Yeah, you need to take responsibility."

Weight-loss is an inside job, it's got to come from within. It doesn't matter what your age is or how many times you exercise, if you want long-term results, it's got to come from inside. Otherwise, it won't stick.

Dave: I think that's where we'll start talking about Gurdeep's question. Before we do, something interesting you talked about was how before you started working full-time in the health and wellness industry you were working your corporate job and then doing fitness coaching on the side. You talked about doing that after hours and that's how I got my start as well.

I know so many other health professionals who do that, but it's sort of hypocritical because we all preach balance, downtime, and helping our bodies de-stress. But working that full-time job and then after hours working that second job because we love health and fitness, but lo and behold your body eventually broke down. I've gone through that as well. Even us fitness professionals aren't immune to overworking or running our bodies down.

Ireene: Oh my goodness, we are so normal. We are absolutely normal. I was working a corporate job working eight, nine, ten hours but then I was training my clients after work, and I was moving. Our bodies are designed to move. You've got to keep moving. To me, it was fun, and I was passionate about helping people. It wasn't work to me.

I was training and meeting with my clients. Showing them, instructing them. For me, it was a form of exercise as well because I was just moving my body.

Dave: One of the things that Gurdeep mentions is she says, "I probably sit 80% of my day." I know that a lot of other business people are working in sedentary jobs. When they read or hear that, they probably think, "Oh geez, I sit at least 80% of my day." What's the first thing that you say to someone who's "forced" into that sedentary lifestyle? How do they even start to break out of that?

HOW DO I MANAGE MY TIME?

Ireene: My first question is what do they do the other 20% of the time because, at the end of the day, time doesn't discriminate. We are all given the same amount of time. I get it, some people have families. Some people travel a long distance for work. At the end of the day, we all have exactly the same amount of time.

You've got to know what you want and why you want it. That's important, which is leads to us using the mind here. It's good to know what you want and why you want it, but does she have a picture of exactly what she wants? Our mind works with pictures.

If Gurdeep wants to excel in her career and do well, what does that look like? Does that look like she is in a trim, taught body looking amazing in her outfits standing up there speaking to people? She's got to really see herself as that person first before she can get it.

If 80% of her time is sedentary, what is she doing with the other 20%? Look at her whole day. Where can she stop and just go for a mini walk? We can all find places to reduce the time we spend like watching TV or how we travel to work. There are many things. The moral of the story is everyone is different. Why I like to work one on one with people is because I like to get an idea of how their life is.

I get my clients to fill out a time diary in fifteen-minute increments as to what they actually do with their entire day because sometimes people can use that as an excuse. I'm not saying Gurdeep is, but people say, "I sit most of the day and then I've got to do other things. Cook dinner and run the kids around or whatever. I don't have the time." You actually do. When you have in your mind exactly what you want, why you want it, and you can see it with a picture, it helps motivate you to find that time.

Dave: You're right. I often talk about the idea of goal-setting or thinking about what our aspirations are. I really like how you talked about it as a picture. How do you suggest people build that picture practically? Is that something they write out? Do they physically draw a picture? How do they do that?

HOW TO VISUALIZE YOUR GOOD HEATH

Ireene: Number one they need to start thinking. A lot of people think that they're thinking, but they're not. We run on autopilot. We just kind of go about our day and let our day run us. We need to stop in the morning say, "This is what I do in the morning." I wake up, and for the first couple of minutes I think, "Wow, what have I got ahead?" I really visualize how I want my day to go.

I visualize myself getting up and eating a really good, healthy breakfast. I see it. Putting on my outfit for the day, or since I work in a gym, I just put on my gym clothes or whatever. I go to the gym, and I go to work. I see people saying hello to me, and I am really happy to see everyone, helping people in the gym.

I see myself throughout the whole day, and I see myself getting everything done I need to. I say as a mantra, as an affirmation, every day: "Everything I need to get done today, I get done with ease."

I make myself see my picture. It's really important that you plant that image in your subconscious mind because what I'm doing there is I'm retraining my mind to think how I want it to think, not let my mind control my day. I take control of my life, not the other way around. Does that make sense?

Dave: Yeah, totally. You just jogged my memory of something. I'm reading a book right now called, *Essentialism*. One of the quotes says, "If you don't prioritize your life, someone else will."

Ireene: So true. In my twenties and early thirties, I let everything else control my life. It was not until I got into my forties I'm like, "You know what? I've got one shot at it, and I don't want to feel like this anymore. I don't want to feel like go, go, go. I want to create my life how I want to lead it."

That was when I decided to work in the health and fitness industry full-time. It's been a long process, and it's something I constantly think about. I visualize and see it. I've now created the life I want. I wanted to live by the beach. I wanted to drive the car that I drive. I wanted my body to look the way it does now. I see it first, and then I just take the steps to get there. It stays constantly in my mind.

We all get sidetracked because of external sources through our five senses. Our smell, touch, sight, hear, and taste.

When you really tap into what you want, your true heart's desire, you ingrain that in your mind. You are focused on that, you create this shield around you like a bubble. You bounce all this other stuff off. You just really stay really focused on where you're going. That's what got me through. I use my mind, and I think. I think about what I want all the time. I know where I'm going.

Like I said, everyone doesn't stop to do that. When it comes to weight-loss, people come to me, and they want to know, "What should I eat?" or "How should I exercise?" Sure, I can give them meal plans or teach them how to eat. That's only short-term. They'll lose weight, but they'll go back to their old ways because they haven't stopped to train their mind.

I'd rather my clients train their mind at first, to start their day by training their mind first because everything else falls into place. Get your mind right first, and then your body will follow.

Dave: It makes a ton of sense. It's interesting reading Gurdeep's question because I really sense a tension there. She sounds like she's ready to make that shift. She's asking the right questions and saying, "Give me some steps." She even says, "I'll check all the boxes." Maybe she will, but there is a tension, unlike you Ireene where you gave up your former career and dove into the health and fitness industry. She says, "You know what? I'm not ready to leave my job, but I want to start making those changes."

For someone like that, what are those baby steps? Where do they start? You talk about train their mind but putting it into practice, how do those two go hand in hand?

PRACTICAL STEPS FOR PRIORITIZING YOURSELF

Ireene: Yeah it's great that she loves her job because we spend so much of our time at work and the people that we work with. If they're negative people, we're going to tend to be negative as well. It's great that she loves her job, she's doing something that she's passionate about.

How do we try to do that? She's got to learn to put herself first. Right now it sounds like she's putting her job first, so she needs to stop. Stop even for a couple of hours and go, "What do I really want and why do I really want it?" Start to write things down.

There's power in writing things down. Gurdeep just really needs to get to know herself better, become her own best friend. Understand what she's thinking and just write down what does she want in all areas of her life? Her career, her health, her relationships, everything. What does she want? Then look at where she is now and where she wants to go. Then slowly just take those steps.

The first step would be like I said, set yourself up with a morning ritual. You get up in the morning and allow yourself the time to visualize for a couple of minutes. Have a good healthy breakfast. If you can do five or ten minutes of some stretching or some yoga, or a five to ten-minute workout to raise your energy, that's great. Get excited about your day. Get excited about your life.

She already loves her job. A lot of people go to jobs that they don't love. She needs to give herself that time in the morning to really focus on her. Eat a lovely breakfast, visualize, do five minutes of movement or exercise and then go and rock it out. Have a great day. When she feels good, she'll be more inclined to make better choices when it comes to food.

I truly believe people need to prepare. Prepare their snacks. Snacks are what lets them down. Most people have breakfast, and they should, but it needs to be a protein-packed breakfast. They need protein with their lunch and protein with their dinner. Where they fall down is the snacks. That takes preparation.

On a Sunday, she could make one or two healthy snacks that have protein in them and make a double batch. Put them in little zip lock bags or freeze them. If you put yourself first, you're preparing, so prepare on a Sunday.

Take your snacks for two, three, four days and then have a treat on a Friday because it's all about 80/20. We're not trying to be 100% perfect here. Gurdeep just needs to take a step back, have a look at her life and put herself first. Think, "What do I want and how am I going to get there?"

If she can't do it on her own—there's a lot of people who don't know how—get help. Seek a mentor. Get someone to help you, because if you want to exceed and excel in your life, most successful people have coaches or mentors to guide them. Follow someone that's already doing it. You don't need to reinvent the wheel. They'll show you the steps.

That's why I love to work with my clients a minimum of three months. I won't work with them for any less because we want to make those new habits stick. They love it because I've guided them and supported them, making them accountable along the way.

PUTTING YOURSELF FIRST DAILY

Dave: Ireene, I've got to jump in there because you gave so many nuggets of truth and I want to highlight a couple. First of all, I love that you said to start in the morning after Gurdeep makes that decision to put herself first. You've probably experienced this with clients who you work with maybe now or when you were a personal trainer, but people will quite often say, "When I exercise, when I'm going to the gym, I naturally choose healthier food options."

It doesn't require some sort of mental gymnastics to get around why that works. When we're treating our bodies the way it needs to be treated, we want to supply it with the fuel that it needs. I love your suggestion to Gurdeep of starting her morning right, and you mentioned some ways to do that.

Creating a morning ritual, you talked about taking a few minutes for a healthy breakfast. Taking a few minutes for exercise. Maybe doing some sort of meditation. If you start your day like that, it's going to be followed by an inclination to make healthier choices for the rest of your day. Is that something you've seen with the clients you work with?

Ireene: Without a doubt. If you follow all successful people, they all start their day off well. They don't just get up and aimlessly have a shower and rush out the door with their hair all messed up. They actually stop and put themselves first by creating what they want. We've really got to take hold of our life. It's time to wake up and not let life control us. If there's something not right in your life, listen to your mind, listen to your body. What is it that you want?

It's setting yourself up by putting yourself first without a doubt. Some women say, "Well I've got three kids. I've got a husband, I've got a full-time job." Sure, I get that. I get that it would be challenging, but you know what? If you want to be your best in all those areas, put yourself first. Only then can you be the best to someone else.

I listen to a lot of different thought leaders like Tony Robbins. He gets up and throws himself into a plunge pool; it's freezing cold. All successful people do start their day off well. Gurdeep is honestly half way there because she loves her job. If she wants to be better at it, just get up ten minutes earlier, visualize, meditate, do some exercise, whatever it might be, but set yourself a morning ritual.

Dave: Okay Ireene, I'm going to put you on the spot here, and I was wondering if you could tell the readers, what does your morning ritual look like?

Ireene: I wake up, and when I realize that I've just woken up I think, "Wow, okay. What's on my day ahead?" I just think for a couple of minutes in the morning.

BUILDING A HEALTHY MORNING RITUAL

Dave: Is this in bed, perhaps before you even get out of bed?

Ireene: I'm lying in bed, and I think, "Okay, what's today? This morning, it's Friday." I got up at a quarter to six. I was eating a healthy breakfast while I was on a webinar. I visualized having this interview with you, and I was really looking forward to it. As soon as I'm done with this interview, I'm then going to be doing a little bit of exercise which I do every morning.

I talk to myself. This might sound crazy—not literally verbalize it—but in my mind, I talk to myself, how I see my day. I've got my appointments scheduled out. I even schedule my gym workouts, which I believe if you make an appointment, you're not going to let yourself down. So I schedule it.

I do a small workout in the morning, but I do a proper workout in the afternoon. I prefer to workout in the afternoon. I don't just visualize it. I see it, and I see what I want to happen. I don't think about what I don't want, I think about what I want to happen. I just see my day because you see it you know what's going to happen. Does that make sense? This stuff is so powerful. This is so powerful, but a lot of people don't do it because it takes works.

Dave: You said something earlier that I think is really important and ties into what we're talking about right now. You mentioned that Gurdeep says, "I probably sit 80% of my day." Right away you reframe that in the positive and say, "Okay, well what's the other 20% look like?"

I can imagine Gurdeep waking up and putting herself first. Going through this mental process of visualizing your day and instead of focusing on all this stuff I need to do at work, thinking, "I have these moments or like glimpses of time when I can get up, and I can move my body. I can make these healthy choices and really own those from the morning and then it will flow through my day."

Ireene: Oh, absolutely. I think about what she does the other 20%? I don't know how she gets to work. Does she sit on a bus or a train or a tram or does she drive to work? Where I work, with the corporate health program, I move my car every two hours because of the parking situation.

People say, "Oh, isn't that a pain in the butt moving your car?" It depends on how you look at it. I love it because it makes me get up and move. I have to walk about four hundred meters to go and move it for another two hours. To me that's a good thing, I'm getting up, and I'm moving my body. I love the fact that I can move my body, where people think, "Oh, I can't be bothered going for a walk. I'd rather just, I don't know, park as close as I can."

Any opportunity that you can go and move your body is good. It depends on how you train your mind. I train my mind always to think forward. Look at the positive. A lot of people stay stuck or think backward; I think forward.

Dave: Ireene, you have such positive thinking. I just imagine if I had to get up and move my car every two hours. I don't know if I'd be looking at the exercise component. I think I'd be frustrated. I love how you've sort of flipped that on its head.

Ireene: Well, I love it because I love moving my body. I know the difference between sitting at a desk all day and not moving. It feels stagnant, and you feel like your waistline is just expanding. You get brain fog. It's just that little, short burst of movement every couple of hours is great for your mind and body.

Dave: So much practical stuff to talk about here. You mentioned creating your goals and creating that picture of where you want to go and looking at different aspects of your life. We talked about this morning ritual and setting your day in the right direction by doing things like making healthy choices right away.

Picturing where your day's going to go. Then you started talking about planning. I liked what you said when you mentioned that, "If you're really putting yourself first, you are going to plan." What are the things that you plan? You mentioned snacks are something that could be planned. What else should people think about planning?

PLANNING AHEAD, DON'T REACT

Ireene: Yeah, food is all about your mindset. When it comes to weight-loss, 80% of it is just food. You can go to the gym and bust your butt, but if you're going home and eating cream cakes, it's not going to work. Food is critical. I always know the day ahead and even probably the following day what I'm going to be eating. My fridge and my pantry are constantly filled with what I want to eat.

Like I said though, if I want to have M&M's, something that's probably not the best thing, I have it. I don't tell myself that I can't have it. I tell myself that if I want it, I can have it, but I choose not to.

It's just planning your food, planning your exercise. I plan in my diary and schedule it like an appointment, every time I work out, which is three or four times a week, I'm in the gym and most days I go for an hour walk.

I look at my appointments and I schedule them, and I highlight my appointments in my diary. I still have a manual diary, not an electronic diary. I can see my day forward, and I see when I'm going to be walking and exercising in the gym.

Then I also plan my mindset training. In the morning I visualize. On my way to work, I listen to something inspirational or motivational. I don't listen to the news or the radio. When I'm walking, I listen to a podcast that's helping me growing my business or helping me become a better person.

I just utilize my time because I believe we're here for a short time. More and more I hear this person has got cancer or so and so's mom just passed away. All these sicknesses and diseases are around so let's just take stock of our lives and make the most of it. Honestly, our life could change in a second.

Dave: The urgency there is such an important message. You said something else that I just want to touch on quickly. You said if you want some M&Ms, you have them. I think it's important to tell the readers you have the ability to do that. You can make that choice to have M&Ms and not worry about the health ramifications because you've planned out your other meals.

I imagine if we did a food diary for you and tracked all of your meals for the week, your meal choices—because they're planned—would be healthy meal choices. Those snacks, indulgences, or treats are okay because that's the 20%. You're already doing the 80%.

The problem quite often is when we don't plan out our meals, then they start to be spur of the moment decisions, or we're starving, so we just grab whatever is easiest. Then we still want those treats, those M&Ms, but we haven't been eating the meals that should have been planned to be healthy meals in the first place. That's where it really starts to become problematic. Is that something you've seen with your clients?

Ireene: Absolutely. I've done it myself. When I haven't put myself first—because like I said we're all normal—it happens to all of us. We'll just grab things on the go. Your body wants more of what you're giving it. If you're giving it sugar and you're giving it crap food, it's going to want more sugar and it's going to want more crap food. Honestly, if you give your body lots of leafy greens and healthy foods, it's going to want more healthy foods.

I pretty much eat the same thing all the time, to be honest. I very rarely steer off, but in the morning it might be oats with protein powder. I might add some chia seeds or flax seeds to it. Then mid-morning I make a green smoothie. I put a bunch of spinach leaves in it with a banana and some frozen berries and have a smoothie.

Every time I eat I ask myself, "What can I add that's protein to this?" You want to add protein to most of your meals. I eat regularly, I eat every two to three hours because your protein—as you know—isn't stored in the body. You need to top it up continually. When you have protein every couple of hours, it keeps you feeling full. You're less inclined to want a sugary snack.

You've got to get to know your body. You've got to tune in to what your body wants. Like I said, when you put yourself first you become your own best friend. You're kind to yourself, and you treat yourself as a priority. Then all this stuff comes easy. Getting a healthy body is easy because I know me. I know my mind, I know me. I understand me. A lot of people don't even know themselves.

Dave: Interesting. You know it's funny that you use the word "priority" again. Until the 1900s, the word "priority" meant singular, one thing. When you said make yourself a priority, that means you are that one thing.

After the 1900s, all of a sudden, we started to morph that word into, "Well, I have my priority list and I'll add it to my priorities." The true meaning of "priority" just goes so strongly hand in hand with your message of, "Put yourself first."

Ireene: You are number one, and that doesn't mean you're being selfish. It's just that there's only one you. Doctor Demartini has "A Valued Determination Process." It's on his website, it's free. People can go to it. It's stating questions to help you identify what your core values are. When you know what your core values are in your life, you make yourself a priority. You set the boundaries. You have your own mission statement, and you just live by that mission statement.

I get all my clients to do that actually. You've got to understand your core values first. What you live and stand for. Then, from there, you'll learn to become a priority. It becomes easier.

Dave: Interesting. For the readers, I'll put a link in the *Resources* section to that. You can go ahead and do it yourself. And who is the doctor again?

Ireene: Doctor John Demartini. The document is called, "A Valued Determination Process." It's free from his website. This is what I mean, follow thought leaders.

The tools and strategies—which is their mindset—that successful people use and makes them successful are the same things you can apply to your body and your health. It's the same thing. It all comes down to mindset.

Dave: I love that, and you've been gracious enough to offer a gift that will maybe help take some of those dreams and put them into action. You're offering a free downloadable planner that you use with your clients and again for the readers, I'll put this in the *Resources* section. You can download a copy of Ireene's planner. Ireene quickly, what does the planner offer or how will that help?

Ireene: The planner is just one page where you write out your meals. Remember how I said you've got to see what way or where you're going? You've written out your meals for the week and your snacks, and there's also an area where you schedule your exercise.

You can also write your top three goals for the week. If it's weight-loss you want, say 500 grams (approximately 1 pound) this week, you'll know in a snapshot exactly where your week is going and where you're heading.

Dave: I'll put it in the *Resources* section. I just love the power of it. One page, fill it out. Have yourself as the priority for the week and then just follow your plan. I think that makes so much sense. Ireene, wow. So much practical advice, so much wisdom here. Thank you so much for being in this interview today.

Ireene: You're most welcome, I loved it. I love talking about this stuff, I could talk about it for hours. I just have to say to all your readers, take control of your mind and don't let your mind take control of you. If you can master the way your mind thinks, you can apply these tools to anything in life, not just weight-loss.

Dave: Awesome. If any of the readers have any questions or want to get in touch with you about the work you do, what's the best way they can reach you?

Ireene: They can go to my website. I'd love to offer your readers a one hour to sit with someone on the phone or one-on-one in Skype to really help you identify all these areas. They can go to my website which is Ireenesiniakis.com.

Dave: I'll put the link right in the *Resources* section again.

Ireene: They can just schedule a consultation with me, one hour. It's not a sales pitch, I just really want to help you take that next step. I don't like people staying stuck, I want to help you take that next step. It's a great opportunity, you should do it.

RESOURCES

Ireene's website: http://www.ireenesiniakis.com

Ireene's "Not Just Weight Loss" Program: https://www.notjustweightloss.com

Dave's Recommended Book: Essentialism by Greg McKeown:
http://makeyourbodywork.com/essentialism

How to Determine Your Values by Dr. Demartini:
http://makeyourbodywork.com/is-values

CHAPTER 4:

DO YOU WANT PROGRESS OR PERFECTION?

Are you a perfectionist?

So many people I've met over the years struggle with their weight or fitness because of perfectionist tendencies. This seems counterintuitive: shouldn't perfectionism lead people to get better results?

Not usually.

Perfection does not exist when it comes to your health. It can be easy to look at yourself and think, "I wish I were just a bit more _____. Then I would be satisfied." If you're like most people, however, satisfaction never comes, or at least doesn't last long, even when you reach what you thought was your end goal.

That's what Kel realized:

> *"I think I'm just a black or white person. When I get into something, it's all I think about. I notice it so much in my life when it comes to food and exercise. I know that I'm healthy already, so I don't need to obsess about every little thing I eat, but I can't help it. The same goes for exercise. If I miss a day or two, I feel miserable and very upset with myself. It's exhausting to constantly feel like I'm evaluating myself. I wish I could just stop, but I don't know how. How can I just be okay with being me?"*

Let me just say that it's great if you want to improve certain areas of your life. I'm all for personal growth. But, how do you feel about yourself right now? Are you okay with "being me" as Kel put it?

MEET JENNIPHER WALTERS

Jennipher Walters is a certified personal trainer and overall health enthusiast. She is the founder of several popular healthy living websites including FitBottomedGirls.com, FitBottomedMamas.com, and FitBottomedEats.com where she inspires women to think past the number on the scale to love themselves for who they are.

She is also the author of *The Fit Bottomed Girls Anti-Diet.*

THE INTERVIEW

Dave: Hey Jennipher, thanks so much for joining me today.

Jennipher: Thank you for having me.

Dave: I don't even know where to begin to describe what you do in the health and fitness industry because I feel like you do everything.

Jennipher: We do a lot.

Dave: So maybe you can start off this way. Tell the readers, what did you get started with? What was your first venture?

Jennipher: In 2008, we started Fit Bottomed Girls. We, being me and my good friend Erin Whitehead. Back then, there weren't a ton of fitness blogs on the scene. And there wasn't a lot of specifically positive body image blogs out there. So, we put out that message, and that's how we started. I feel like we're super-old in internet years. 2008 is so like dog years. We're like 100.

But it took off and gained momentum. We got lucky and built a community, letting women know they are more than a number on the scale, which wasn't a message they were getting in mainstream media. At least not at that time. And still not entirely today, but certainly not then.

In 2010, we launched Fit Bottomed Mamas when Erin got pregnant with her first kid. She now has three.

Dave: So, you're going to follow your lifestyle as you guys go through different stages of life?

Jennipher: Yes. We just keep building and growing.

In 2014, we launched Fit Bottomed Eats because our nutrition content at Fit Bottomed Girls blew up because cooking and healthy eating were so popular. Now, we're starting FitBottomedZen.com, which is a lot of mind-body meditation, improving your life and self-confidence kind of thing.

It's been a natural progression as we've gotten more into it and seen a need. All of our sites have a strong mission, like always having a positive body image. Always about improving your life. But each of those sites has their unique twist on an area of life.

Dave: I was going to say, you've come full-circle. Fit Bottomed Girls, like you just described, initially started from a place of acceptance. And now, you're topping off with a site devoted to mental well-being.

Jennipher: We have a new business partner who came on with us, Kristen, last January. So, Erin, Kristen, and I have all personally gotten more into the meditation site, how to boost confidence, and how to be well.

ADOPTING A POSITIVE BODY IMAGE

As we've all learned, nutrition is super-important. Workouts are super-important too. Whichever way your lifestyle is set up, it's crucial for your health. If you can get the mental, stress, and time management sides all taken care of, it's much easier to find the time and have energy to workout. To eat right and cook and do all the other things you want to do.

So, being a Fit Bottomed Girl—or as you are a Fit Bottomed Dude—it's not just about going to the gym and eating right. It's truly a lifestyle that supports your life's purpose.

Dave: I couldn't agree more. I've had a question in the past from someone—her name was Joy—who was exercising like crazy and wasn't seeing any results. We talked about the idea of being kind to your body. It's more than just eating and exercise.

Jennipher: It is. It really is.

Dave: The question today is from Kel. I know when you and I chatted via email, you thought this one is perfect for you. Kel says she's a black and white person. She is hardcore. She is into exercising and eating and just can't stop. But then if she falls off track, she kicks herself and gets down on herself. Is this something, through your relationships with people who visit your site and your community, you see often?

Jennipher: Yeah. Kel's experience is common. An all-in, all-out mentality. The on-again, off-again relationship is so common. I experienced the same thing: over exercising and under eating. Then next week I would say I'm going to do it even harder and better. But then I couldn't sustain it because it's not realistic. That's something I had gone through before we started Fit Bottomed Girls.

I pulled myself together and made peace with that, realizing I was more than the number on the scale. I thought about why I was torturing myself like that. That is not the way to live. This is part of the foundation Fit Bottomed Girls is built on.

HOW JENNIPHER MADE PEACE WITH THE SCALE

Dave: Before you get into it, can you tell us a little bit more about your story? Why do you think you were going through that?

Jennipher: Yeah. I believe it's because of culture and society, specifically for women. It targets men too, and I feel like the pressure is getting harder on men more than it used to. But for women, we are told so many times what you look like is where you should derive your worth, your self-value, and your self-confidence.

When you're growing up, in your teens, your twenties, and even when you're older, these issues linger. They affect your self-esteem. For myself, I always put my power in my weight and my appearance. I like to workout. I like to eat right. I thought I was doing the right things. I started teaching group exercise classes in college, and I loved it.

I loved it so much I got into personal training. But I had some negative body image going on. It was a result of being told over and over again, "You'll be a better person, prettier, all the guys will like you, and get the job of your dreams if you lose 10 pounds."

Once I started working in the fitness industry, no one else was putting pressure on me to look a certain way besides myself. But I felt like, to give fitness advice, I needed to look a certain way.

Dave: I'm in a fitness competition with a guest of mine from a previous interview and she's getting ready for a photo shoot. She's a fitness competitor.

If you look at her, you think she's got the dream body. She is in such great shape. But she said that she looks like that for only one day. It's just for photo day or competition day. And she gets so miserable; she can't wait until the photo shoot finishes so she can be normal again.

Jennipher: I don't want to live that way.

Dave: No.

Jennipher: You know? That does not sound fun to me. I would much rather have a slice of pizza and a glass of wine a couple of times a week than have the perfect body. The pressure is so real. So, when I was going through that, I was over-exercising. I was under-eating.

Then I would be starving. I would be so hungry because of everything I was doing: constant cardio and not eating enough. Then I would go completely off whatever crazy diet plan I was following and eat a ton. Then I'd feel bad about myself, every single time. Every time I did it, I would go for something more extreme, and then I would fail.

When you think you're repeatedly failing, your self-confidence tanks. So, while it was tanking, I had to step outside myself and say, "Jenn, guess what? You don't suck. What you're doing sucks. Your diet sucks. You're good. But this whole dieting thing, over-exercising thing, it's not working for anyone. It's not working for you. That's the problem, not you as a person."

Dave: Sorry Jenn, can I just stop you? I just want to emphasize that point again. Readers, this is so true. Being able to separate yourself from your actions or whatever is going on in your life is crucial. It isn't you. Great message.

Jennipher: Yeah. It's not you. That's why we wrote a whole book, called "The Fit Bottomed Girls Anti-Diet" because dieting is so detrimental to health.

Diets are always about deprivation, and they're always on-again-off-again. If you go on a diet, you always come off a diet. But what happens is you lose all of your self-confidence, which is where I was. My rock bottom moment was planning for my wedding, which was a great moment, don't get me wrong.

Dave: Glad you clarified that.

Jennipher: But when I started to do my wedding planning and bought my dress, I started thinking about the day. I did not want to walk down the aisle worrying if my arms looked fat, if I fit in my dress, or how the pictures would look.

I wanted to be in the moment. I wanted to be present. I didn't want to be in my head about my appearance on what is supposed to be one of the best days of my life. That's stupid. I wasn't going to start this new chapter of life like that.

So, I met with a registered dietitian who specializes in emotional eating and intuitive eating. Our first meeting, she asks, "Can you imagine what the women of this world could do if they stopped worrying about the number on the scale?"

Dave: A lot of extra energy they'd spend elsewhere.

Jennipher: Yes! And that hit me like a ton of bricks because I felt like such an idiot. I had never thought of that before. I never thought about that potential I have with all my energy. And what am I doing? I'm spending all my mental energy counting calories. Are you kidding me? There is more to life than counting calories.

STOP EXPECTING PERFECTION

So, with her help, journaling, and lots of self-care practices, I stopped over-exercising. I started eating regular amounts of food. No foods were off-limits. I got in touch with my hunger and fullness cues, which took me months.

But, I stopped fighting myself, and I began to trust myself, getting back in touch with my body. When you stop expecting perfection from yourself, you realize you're fine as you are. You start making choices because you love yourself. That's when everything changes.

Through that experience and talking with Erin about them, finding workouts we liked, putting the fun back in fitness and in healthy eating, we stopped focusing on diets or deprivation. That's where the mission comes from. So, when you get a question like that, I know it.

Dave: Yeah you do.

Jennipher: I know it. I know it hard.

Dave: Honestly, the story you explained is what Kel's specifically talking about. You said a lot of stuff I want to unpack. First, you talked about your book. Is it the anti-diet?

Jennipher: Yeah. The Fit Bottomed Girls Anti-Diet.

DEVELOPING YOUR PEACE WITH THE SCALE

Dave: You also talked about the idea of not focusing on the numbers on the scale, but loving yourself and being okay with yourself. Those are both fantastic concepts. How can those play out in real life?

Jennipher: How do you do that? Yes. That's the deep part. I think the first step is being aware of your head space and what you're saying to yourself. We say, talk to yourself like your best friend. That's easy to say, but that is harder to do. But the first step is paying attention to what you are saying to yourself.

Because I think a lot of us just go through life beating ourselves up without ever stopping and thinking, Did I just think that? That's not appropriate. I wouldn't say that to someone else. Why would I say that to myself?"

I think awareness is key. And it may be something as simple as setting the alarm on your phone, where every hour it goes off and for 20 seconds check-in with yourself and say, "Remember, we're treating ourselves with love today. We're respecting ourselves."

We're talking to ourselves like our best friend. We get into habits with thoughts. We wake up, have a negative thought that we don't look good or something.

Then you do it again. Then those thoughts turn into emotions. Once you start having emotions, you're acting upon them. If you act upon them enough times, you build habits. If you want to improve anything, starting with the thought process is number one.

REPURPOSING YOUR SCALE

I also recommend—and this is in our book—these 10-minute fixes to ditch dieting. But one of my favorites is to repurpose your scale. Make it a little dream board with pictures and sayings on it; we call it "Reclaim the scale." On mine, some say, "You're gorgeous darling."

Something fun. And a woman meditating. Images that bring me joy. I have a picture of a little sheep because I like sheep. I want to see my scale and smile. Sheep make me smile. So, put your flair on it. Then when you see your scale, it's no longer a mortal enemy, it's just a thing.

Dave: Yeah. I like that. There is an importance in being able to see progress. I think in the fitness industry we tend toward using the scale because it's objective. It's easy to see that number.

The number changes. Therefore, you must be doing something right, even if it's not the case. Since you're moving clients away from the scale, what do you teach as another barometer for success?

Jennipher: It depends on where your relationship is with the scale. Some women can get on and aren't overly bothered by it. They're okay with wherever they are. If that's you and you don't obsess over it, that's cool. Weigh in every couple days, every week, every couple weeks, or whatever you want to do.

If you are someone who has a past like me where the number is flashing at you, and it determines your mood for the day, then put it under the bed, in the closet. Do not weigh yourself 2, 3, 4 times a day. Get away.

Instead, go by how your clothes feel. That's always a good way. Or a simple tape measure, $2. Then measure different areas on your body. Measure around your belly button, hips, arms, or legs.

Dave: Again, without doing it 4 times a day. You can do once a week or every other week or something.

Jennipher: Right. Because that's going to take longer to change. So, write those numbers down. It can be your starting point. But if you need to focus your energies on tracking something, track how you feel.

Maybe your goal isn't to lose a bunch of weight. Maybe your goal is to feel good. I think that's what we're all striving for.

Dave: You know, the way I like to say it is, everyone wants to be happier. If losing weight will make you happy, maybe that's the case.

Jennipher: Maybe not.

Dave: Maybe it's something else tied to the fitness process.

Jennipher: Exactly. I always want people to find their why. Take out a piece of paper and write down why you want to lose weight? Or why do you want to get fit? Why do you want to be healthy? And keep asking yourself why. Is it because you want to look hot in a swimsuit. Why do you want that?

Dave: You are preaching to the choir. You used to be a personal trainer, so I'm sure you went through this intake process with someone. Pretty much everyone who comes into a personal trainer says they want to lose weight.

You go through the process of asking why and you find out the underlying cause. It is typically so removed from just changing the number on the scale. It's usually something much deeper. But without going through the process, you have no idea.

Jennipher: Exactly and today, maybe it has nothing to do with working out or eating right. Maybe it has to do with a difficult conversation, standing up for yourself, or starting your day in a different way.

Once you start to feel better, you'll have some energy. Then do a workout that supports your goal, instead of beating yourself to death in the gym with something you hate to do and then you hate your life.

IT'S TIME TO GIVE YOURSELF A PEP TALK

Dave: I couldn't agree more. So Kel is explaining exactly the idea of beating yourself up. Her exact words were, "You know, if I miss even a day or two," then she starts getting down on herself. You brought up the point, be kind to yourself, remind yourself you are good. You can love yourself just as you are. What else can someone do—specifically regarding exercise—to avoid falling into the thinking of if they miss a day, they're a bad person?

Jennipher: I think it's critical to get out of the weeds and see the whole forest. She's in the mental habit of needing to do this or needing to do that. And if she doesn't, she is going to fall off. What that says to me is she's doesn't trust herself enough. She feels like if she doesn't do something, then it's all going to be lost.

I think sometimes you just have to sit down and say, "It's going to be okay. You missed two days; it's going to be fine." Fitness, healthy living isn't going anywhere, you know?

A lot of times, I'll even have clients write themselves a love letter. Maybe if she just took a few minutes and wrote a letter to herself or a reassurance message? That's something she could go back and look at later in times where she's trying to beat herself up.

If you're having trouble writing it, have a friend or loved one, someone supportive, and you've shared some these struggles with. Have them help you with the letter or even have them write you a letter.

Dave: I love that idea, particularly, if it was dated. I could imagine someone having this letter from a month ago, and then went 2 days without exercising. Then they realize, "I didn't fall apart, I'm still in just as great a shape as I was a month ago." It's like proof of concept. Missing a day or two is okay.

Jennipher: Exactly. You got this. It'd be like your own pep talk.

Dave: That's so powerful. Kel talks about food as well. You, me, everyone all go through these issues. We eat poorly or fall off our plan. Again, mindset-wise, what do you suggest for people to do in those cases?

DO YOU REALLY LOVE YOUR FOOD?

Jennipher: I think a lot about the all or nothing mindset. It's not a complicated issue, yet it is complicated because it's multi-faceted. I think some of it is hunger and fullness cues. A lot of times, if you've been into yo-yo dieting, you rarely eat because you're hungry and you rarely stop when you're full.

Instead, you eat because the plan says so or you don't eat even though you're hungry. It puts when to eat and how much to eat in the hands of someone else instead of your own body.

I use the scale of 1 to 10 for hunger. Zero or 1 is, "I'm going to eat my arm off," and 10 is like, "I'm so full, I had Thanksgiving dinner like 5 times." You want to eat when you're at a 3 or 4 hunger level. Then you want to stop when you're at a 7, 7.5, somewhere in there. If you can just check in before you eat, when you're eating, after eating.

And you don't have to be perfect with it. Perfect is not the point. The point is not to always be at a 3 and then at a 7. The point is to learn about yourself. Am I full? Am I hungry? What does that feel like? Then wiggle around and see what that's like. Then make it a practice, rather than an all-in thing.

The scale was critical for helping me. The other crucial thing was to ensure I always had a little protein, fiber, and fat, in each snack and meal I had. For so long, I would always binge on carbs.

Then I would be starving afterward because if you don't have enough protein and fat in your diet, you're never satiated. I was never satiated. Adding more of those things in, having more balanced meals and snacks helped me feel more fulfilled.

When you're used to constantly being starving or stuffed, it's nice to be a place where you can say, "I'm not hungry. I feel fulfilled. I feel good."

The third thing I do is a 10-minute—or just 5-minutes—chocolate meditation to help with mindful eating.

Dave: This sounds dangerous.

Jennipher: It's fantastic. You take a small piece of dark chocolate and set a timer for 5 minutes. Then you slowly take 5 minutes to eat that little piece of dark chocolate. It's amazing how, when you're mindful and present, after a couple of minutes, the chocolate doesn't taste as good.

When you're done with it, you're like, "I'm satisfied with one piece of chocolate." But, if you're an emotional eater, it can also be an excellent time to bring up issues.

Maybe just having a piece of chocolate in your hand is enough to make you anxious or want to gobble it up right now. You just breathe through that. It's a way to observe yourself. Not judge yourself. Just observe, learn, and grow.

Dave: That's very reminiscent of Deepak Chopra. He talks about mindfulness. I remember watching him give a talk once. He had a glass of water sitting on the table, and he talked about how he was very thirsty.

Instantly, we just want to grab that glass. And he says, "I'm just thinking about what it will feel like to pick up the glass." And he picks it up. Then I think about what it's going to be like to touch the glass to my lips. It's a painful process to watch, but boy does it make you mindful of when the water starts going into your mouth.

Jennipher: It does. Yeah. It's a heightened experience. So many of us say, "I love to eat." But are you bringing love to your relationship with food? When you sit down to dinner, is there any love on the plate? Or is it just like, "Ugh, I have to eat this."

Or, "I better eat every single French fry in sight because God knows I'm never going to let myself have French fries again."

Instead, when you take the limit of good foods and bad foods off, you can say, "I'm going to have a couple of fries now. If I want fries again tomorrow, I'll have a couple more fries. But I'm not going to eat so many I feel sorry."

Dave: You know, I love your message about the anti-diet. A message I like to convey is if you ever see something billed as the one-size fits all diet, run away because everyone is so unique it's impossible ever to be true.

Jennipher: And there wouldn't be as many diets on the market if they worked. It just doesn't make any sense. If they're all claiming to be the best thing ever, there should only be one.

Dave: Exactly. Your approach of awareness takes more work because we're not just following a set plan, instead, we're tuning in, thinking about where we are on the fullness scale, how we feel after eating certain foods and journaling. Yeah, it's a lot of work for 4 or 6 weeks. But guess what? You have a plan that works for you.

IT'S TIME TO RECOGNIZE HOW YOU FEEL

Jennipher: Yeah. That's what's empowering. It's not anyone else telling you what to do. It's you listening to yourself, respecting yourself, and loving yourself. It's a very loving process to say, "Self, what do you want today? Okay, that's what we're going to do." Then following through. Use how you feel as a guide. Then you never go off track because you're in charge of it.

You don't have to rebel against anything. I used to rebel against all kinds of rules. Choose your adventure. Use your life as an experiment. When you do the work, later on, it's easy to go to the gym. And it's easy to turn down unhealthy food because you know it makes you feel terrible and it's not worth it.

Dave: Yeah. It's a process. At first, there are going to be barriers, and it will be hard to break some of those habits. I liked how you spoke about people eating because it's a particular time of day or because of social cues saying it's time to eat. It's hard getting through the barriers. But once we break through them, it gets easier.

Jennipher: Yeah. It is emotional work. Back in the day, my obsession with calorie-counting, over-exercising, and the number on the scale was merely a reflection of my lack of self-confidence. I took those feelings and my anxiety, and I channeled it toward my obsession. Some people deal with other things in other ways, clearly. But for me, I was addicted to the on-again-off-again. That's where it was challenging. But once I defeated that, I got my power back.

Dave: I love this. You know, Jennipher, for readers out there, if they want to find out more about what you do, what's the best place they can connect with you?

Jennipher: Yeah. Fitbottomedgirls.com, Fitbottomedmamas.com, Fitbottomedeats.com, and Fitbottomedzen.com. Then we're on social media all over the place, and Twitter @Fitbottomedgirl.

Dave: Perfect and I'll put links in the *Resources* section. Check out all these sites; they're fantastic. You post some really great content and always have. Very inspiring message.

Jennipher: Thank you for chatting. I loved it.

RESOURCES

Below are links to the websites that make up Jennipher's "Fit Bottomed World:"

Fit Bottomed Girls: http://fitbottomedgirls.com

Fit Bottomed Mamas: http://fitbottomedmamas.com

Fit Bottomed Eats: http://fitbottomedeats.com

Fit Bottomed Zen: http://fitbottomedzen.com

CHAPTER 5:

ARE YOU IN THE "FAILED DIETERS" CLUB?

Put up your hand if you belong to the "Failed Dieter's Club."

This club is home to anyone who has taken up a diet plan but fell off-track before reaching the intended end goal.

Membership in this club is far too large to count, and many members have joined and re-joined dozens of times, each time hoping that this will be their last diet.

As we discussed in the last chapter, diets rarely, if ever, work. But, there's something seductive about the newest diet. Maybe this is the one that will finally help you lose those ten pounds? Maybe this one is easier than all the others you've tried?

Cassie is part of this club, and she wants out:

> *"Over many years, I have done macrobiotics, low fat, high fat, Paleo, bulletproof, vegetarian, Weston A. Price, and now somebody's trying to push me towards isogenic. I've never thought of myself as a fad dieter, but looking at that list, clearly I am.*
>
> *Initially, all these different ways of eating have been successful but never have been entirely sustainable. After all these years of different styles of eating, I don't know which way is up anymore.*
>
> *I just want to be healthy and follow a sensible plan, but what does that even mean? What does a healthy diet actually look like?"*

You don't have to be a victim of fad diets any longer. Let's discuss how you can break that cycle of on-again-off-again dieting.

Meet Jenn Pike

Jenn Pike is a Registered Holistic Nutritionist who helps women achieve their health and fitness goals. She holds numerous certifications, including yoga instructing and health coaching.

She writes magazine articles, has a best-selling book, and hosts multiple televisions shows where she shares the good news of living a holistic and healthy lifestyle.

The Interview

Jenn: Thank you for having me, I'm excited.

Dave: Yeah, you and I met a couple of months ago, at a fitness conference. As soon as I heard you speak about your business and what you do, I thought, "Okay, I need to get an interview with this girl." I was wondering if you could start by telling the readers about yourself. What are your specialties and what you do in the fitness industry?

Jenn: My name is Jenn Pike, and I'm a holistic lifestyle expert. I've been in the industry for almost 20 years; I feel I've worn nearly every hat there is. I still do some personal training, and I'm a yoga instructor, but my main passion is nutrition. I'm a best-selling author of *The Simplicity Project*. My book is about taking what overwhelms you, the stress, and the complication out of what it means to be healthy and feel vital in your body.

Primarily, I work with women and moms who feel overwhelmed by trying to adopt new habits and be healthy in their body. I've got a show called *Simplicity TV* which teaches people how to cook, how to move, how to feed and nourish their body, and balance hormones.

Dave: That's awesome. When I got this question from Cassie, I thought, "This is perfect for Jenn." She listed all these different diets she's tried, and I believe she's doing the opposite of what you preach. She's making it so complicated by trying to incorporate all of these ideas. What do you think when you read her comment?

Jenn: That that's the most common question I get because it's what so many people are doing. We live in a day and age where there's no lack of information; there's a surplus. It's so difficult to sort through it when it's not your first language, and it's not what you do for a living, even if you are in the industry.

You can't even stand in the grocery store, paying for your food, without being bombarded by 5 different magazine covers selling you 5 different diets you should do this week. I feel for Cassie and where she is coming from. I totally understand.

There's no black or white information; I always say there's gray information. There's a lot of good information out there, but there's also a lot of not-so-good information out there. How do you figure out, for your personal body and your life, what's going to work best for you?

Dave: I love what you just closed with there, the idea of how do you figure out for you? I stress that everyone is unique. But that adds to the complication, because if we're all unique, how do you know what's best for you? What are the first steps? How do people figure it out?

HEALING YOUR DIGESTIVE SYSTEM

Jenn: The first steps are getting to the foundation of your personal health. No matter who you are, or what your age is, it always comes down to your digestion. It's not just about what you're putting in your body, but how well you are breaking it down. Do you eat food and feel energized after? Do you feel like you can still move throughout your day? Or, do you eat food and feel tired and bloated, gassy, lethargic? Do you get a headache afterward?

Come back to the core aspect of healing your digestion first. Start there. One of the tips I thought of immediately for Cassie was to pay attention to her body signals, as opposed to what she is told she shouldn't and should be eating.

Our bodies are whispering—and sometimes yelling—all day long to us. If we stop for a moment and listen to ourselves as the guide and the teacher, it's pretty amazing what you can learn.

Dave: I've had some clients who have come to me and said, "Hey, I've done a food journal." The common pop culture, fitness, and wellness, "Do a food journal, see what you're eating." Then, they ask, "What am I supposed to do with this?" What do you suggest to clients? What should they be tracking regarding what they're eating and how they're feeling? What should they look for?

Jenn: I call it a food and mood journal. I use it with my clients all the time, and it's in my book. I don't ever ask people to count their calories, fat, protein, or carbs. I'm not worried about that. I want to know what they're eating and how they felt after that. Throughout the day, what was their energy like? What was their digestion like? What was their mood like?

How many bowel movements did you have? Were you hydrated? For me, a journal is a lens to take a look at the bigger picture of what's happening within their body. If we're always focusing on the caloric density of food versus the macronutrients and micronutrients—where all of our nutrition actually is—we're missing the whole point.

Dave: Yeah, totally. Again, to make this practical for our readers and Cassie, if you're reading right now, not only record what you're eating but also record how your body is feeling and how it's affecting your psychology, your mood. What sort of timeline do you recommend? Should someone do this for 1 day, for 3 days, for a week?

Jenn: I would say 4 days to a maximum of 7. We're creatures of habit. The reality is, with clients, by the time I get to day 4, I pretty much know what they're eating every single day.

Dave: Isn't that true? We're creatures of habit.

Jenn: Yeah.

Dave: Even I'd say that of myself, and probably for you as well?

Jenn: Oh, yeah. We are. We're creatures of habits. When something feels like it starts to work, we're like, "Well, why change it?" It becomes easy and not so complicated. For someone like Cassie, I feel like she is at the point where keeping a journal for a few days is a good idea.

IS IT TIME TO GET PROFESSIONAL ADVICE?

But, then I think she needs to sit across from somebody, a holistic nutritionist or someone in the industry. Someone who can be the unbiased and objective eyes to peer in and help her decipher all this information she has. It sounds like she's trying a lot of things at once.

Dave: Agreed, agreed. The idea of getting a third party, someone who has objective opinions or advice is great. I remember when I did an IgE blood test for food sensitivities years ago. I remember getting the results back, and it's funny because I didn't want to believe what they were telling me. I instantly started to rationalize, "I can still eat almonds because of this and this." When you have those emotions and your preferences tied into it, it's very hard to create an action plan.

Jenn: It is. Although I work in the industry, I still have a personal trainer, coach, naturopath, homeopath, and chiropractor. That's their specialty and their scope of practice. We start to justify ourselves because, typically, with food sensitivities and allergies, it's your favorite foods that pop up the most.

Dave: Yes, it is.

Jenn: Right? It's because when you overeat the same thing time and time again, your body never gets an opportunity to replenish the enzymes required to break it down. You've overworked your system, and it finally throws up the white flag. It gets ticked off at you and is like, "I can't digest this anymore. I've digested it for the last 140 days straight; I'm done."

Dave: That's a depressing message for everyone out there listening right now. They're probably thinking, "Oh geez, that means I can't eat X, Y, Z." Does that mean people have to cut out those foods they've developed a sensitivity to for the rest of their lives?

Jenn: Not the rest of their lives. Every person is different, so for some people, we can remove it for a month and then introduce it back in. But don't reintroduce it daily. Have it here and again.

FOOD ROTATION: ENSURE SOME VARIETY ON YOUR PLATE

Ultimately, you want variety on your plate. That way you guarantee yourself varying nutrients, a different number of calories each day, and different vitamins and minerals. The importance of variety goes beyond food sensitivity.

Dave: A tactic I want my clients to adopt is an idea of having go-to meals for each mealtime throughout the day. It's easy to get into a routine and eat the same breakfast, but if there are 3 breakfasts you rotate through—and as long as those 3 have different ingredients—in theory, you shouldn't develop those sensitivities of over consuming the same food.

Jenn: Absolutely. Many people drink smoothies, and they're great. But you find people end up doing the same smoothie: spinach, blueberries, flax seed, almond milk, and the same protein powder. And they do that forever, and ever.

This meal could be so healthy and had them feeling great in the beginning, but now has left them feeling bloated, or cravings afterward. They're not satisfied. It's not the smoothie, it's what's going in it. It's just changing up some of the variables; it doesn't mean you have to cast it away entirely.

Dave: Can you speak to that a little bit more? Food rotation is what we're talking about right now. For any of the readers who want to add some variety, should they be trying to do something different every day for 3 days, 5 days, or 7 days? Could they do a week at a time? How does that work?

Jenn: I used to do plans for people based on 7 days. The reality was, nobody can do something different for 7 days. You can't wake up on Monday, and this is what you eat today, this is what you eat Tuesday. Food is left over, so you have carry-over.

It's also not realistic in our schedules to think we're going to eat something different every single day of the week and then prepping that food. I find 3 and 4-day rotations work well for people because they can start the cycle again. You're only repeating for a 3 or 4-day rotation for 4 to 6 weeks at a time and then you change again.

Like you said, choose 3 breakfasts that are easy, 3 or 4 lunches and dinners. But I try and leave as much open space as possible for dinner usually because that's when we come together as a family, so there are more mouths you're trying to satisfy.

Then, your snacks, which I refer to as ammunition. They'll load you up and keep you supported and protected, or they'll take you down. You need to have a couple of those things. Have a handful or 2 suggestions of snacks that work for your body. If you focus on consistently rotating, your body will start to crave the good stuff more often.

HOW TO APPROACH MEAL PLANNING

Dave: It all comes down to self-awareness and some planning.

Jenn: The planning is critical. There's no magic bullet. There's no supplement or food product in the store that's going to do the work for you. It's about becoming educated, such as reading books like this. As a nutritionist, I can put together what I think is the most incredible meal plan, but me sliding a plan across the table to you and telling you what to do without educating you on why isn't helpful.

Until you understand the reasoning behind it, it's not going to hold the same weight, and you're going to feel like how Cassie's feeling. Feeling like she has to follow plan after plan. Often, when people slow it down and are more patient, they learn more along the way. Then those habits become part of who we are and what we do. It's no longer a program.

Dave: I appreciate that. So wise. I hesitate to tell this story. When I first started out in the industry, I remember the first meal plan I ever made for a client. I took all of my favorite meals and put it together and said, "Here's what you should eat."

Jenn: I think we've all done that.

Dave: I remember coming back a week later, and she said—in a nice way— "Dave, I hated this plan." It was such a learning opportunity for me. People have different taste buds, different needs, and what works for you isn't going to work for me. It's got to be individualized.

Jenn: Yeah. That's what it comes down to. Us as practitioners have to listen to the individual that's talking.

SYMPTOMS ONLY YOU CAN FEEL

So often we think we need another test done. We have to find out what this benchmark is, and what this is. The symptomatology of how we feel every day manifests from the time you get out of bed and make your way to the washroom, looking in the mirror, putting on your clothes, to how you interact with everyone throughout the day.

Those signs and symptoms, you're not going to be able to see in a blood test or on a medical diagnostic; that's something that only you can feel.

When you start to describe yourself by words like, "I'm exhausted all the time. I'm wired but tired. I'm this. I'm that." You're feeling frustrated because nothing is coming back in your lab work. Your answers are in words you're using to describe yourself.

That is powerful information for me as a practitioner because although I do blood analysis, and I look at all of that, I'm more concerned with how're you feeling. Tell me the way you feel now, how does that show up in your work? How does that show up in your relationship? How does that show up in your parenting? How we feel in one thing shows up in everything.

Dave: I couldn't agree more. The problem with this is it's not a black and white solution.

Jenn: Exactly.

Dave: People—myself included—want blood work done, and I want them to say, "Eat these 20 foods and don't eat these 20 foods." But, it doesn't work that way.

Jenn: Yeah. Sometimes you have to take that approach working with certain clients. I work, primarily, with women and children, and sometimes I have to create a plan based on that personality, where I have to say, "Okay, this is what you are going to eat." But I know in the back of my mind, in our next phase working together, I'm going to switch it up.

For some people, if they're so overwhelmed and crave certainty, they can't be left at the helm deciding what they're supposed to eat. You have to create a more linear approach in the beginning. Then, once they feel good and their confidence in their body's ability and their own at preparing food and being in the kitchen, then I find they're more apt to take on more responsibility.

Dave: Again, 100% agreed. Back to Cassie and everyone reading. I think a lot of people are going to be able to relate to her question. You've given some excellent advice: start looking at what you're eating, how that makes you feel, and think about variety in you're eating. What would be the next step? Imagine she looks at her food journal for the past 3, 4, 7 days, and says, "Okay, I realize these patterns." Do you think to cut out foods right away? I could see it being a haphazard process.

INTRODUCE NEW FOOD, CUT OUT WHAT YOU DON'T NEED

Jenn: I do a bit of both. I have been that practitioner who just went in and identified everything that needed to be cut out. Over the years, it's more effective if you introduce new, delicious, great foods before you start to pull things away from them automatically.

Now, it's different if there were something I felt was the culprit. Often dairy is a huge one, especially because I'm working with a lot of hormonal and digestive issues. I find if we pull out cow's milk, and yogurt, and excessive amounts of cheese throughout the day, the bowels become more balanced, skin starts to calm down, and the level of overall mucous and inflammation in the sinuses settles.

I also want to get my clients hydrated immediately, and I want to increase their plant-based foods. I want to get more greens in; I want there to be more natural color coming into their diet than artificial.

Typically, that's where I go. Sometimes it's going to be gluten and various grains I cut. We have a massive population which, from over consumption, is so carbohydrate and insulin sensitive. That doesn't mean carbs as a food group is the issue. It's the source and how we're preparing it.

Dave: Again, I couldn't agree more. A question for you regarding these big sensitivity offenders, like gluten or dairy. Do you find your clients' reaction or the symptoms show up immediately following consumption? For example, if Cassie was sensitive to dairy, would she say, "I feel bad X number of hours after eating."

UNDERSTANDING FOOD SENSITIVITY

Jenn: If it's an acute sensitivity, meaning it's relatively new in the body, typically the reaction is within anywhere from 30 minutes to 36 hours of consumption. It will usually be immediate. Symptoms are the stomach not feeling well, bloating, gassy, either constipated or congested. Those types of things will happen.

If it's somebody who has a sensitivity over a prolonged period, they probably don't recognize a sensitivity. To them, having a headache, feeling like crap, being constipated, having eczema is just part of what they consider their identity now. They no longer see that as weird, or unnatural. They just think that's their body. It's different for everyone.

I've worked with some clients, more specifically with things like gluten and corn, where if they are around someone who's consuming it, it's airborne, or they touch it, they immediately get a reaction. When you're working with somebody who has severe reactions, we're normally dealing with leaky gut. That's permeable and a deeper issue. That takes more time to heal.

For most people, if we start by cleaning up the big offenders, then we add more incredible plant-based foods, hydrate their body, and get healthy, good fat in their system. I notice huge results in people.

Dave: I love how you talked about the spectrum of time when people can expect to see, or maybe not even notice, the symptoms. I've worked with tons of clients who experience bloating all the time or being exhausted all the time. Like you said, that's their identity, their life. They don't even know there's something better anymore.

Jenn: That's when doing an elimination becomes powerful. It's really cool. You can remove a food for up to 72 to 96 hours—3 to 4 days—and that helps. But people think they have to remove it for a full month to know if it's bothering them.

For example, someone will cut a food for 3 or 4 days, and then I reintroduce it. Almost every single time they will email or call me, and say, "I can't believe it, I got a headache immediately," or, "My congestion came back and my nose started to run again." That's not me telling them they have a sensitivity; that's them not able to ignore the symptoms their body was trying to tell them all along. They just never took a long enough pause to listen.

THE BIGGEST FOOD OFFENDERS

Dave: Off the top of your head, could you list some of those biggest offenders. I could imagine someone thinking, "I'd like to do this, I'd like to remove something and do that test." What should they start with? You mentioned gluten and dairy.

Jenn: I think gluten, dairy, corn, and eggs are going to be a big offender for quite a few people. Citrus foods tend to show up a lot as well. Oranges, strawberries, and green peppers as well. I've never worked with a client whose sensitivity testing didn't reveal green peppers. Cantaloupe is another one because the skin has the same protein as ragweed.

Another interesting thing with sensitivities is a lot of our environment is a factor. It's making its way into our system not just by breathing it airborne outside, but also in foods.

Our plant-based foods are falling from trees and growing from the earth, so they're affected as well. Obviously, the number of genetically modified foods are increasing, so reduce your exposure to those and artificial sweeteners. Chocolate, unfortunately for a lot of people tends to be—

Dave: Oh, no.

Jenn: Yeah, I know.

Dave: You just made enemies.

Jenn: One reason chocolate shows up is it's high in tyramine, which is a trigger for migraines and headaches. Also, most chocolate is milk chocolate, so is it the dairy and the sugar that's causing you the issue, or is it the chocolate?

If you can have cacao and you're fine, then chocolate is not your issue. It's all the sugar and dairy added to it creating the problem.

Dave: Yeah. Oh, fantastic. That's really helpful. That list gives everyone something they can start with.

WHAT FOOD CRAVINGS MEAN

Jenn: I would also ask people, what do you crave most? Our cravings are massive indicators for us in 1 of 2 ways. Either you're craving what you're deficient in, or you're craving your body's form of a drug—like crack—the thing that is actually irritating it the most.

As a mom, when you have children—this goes for fathers too—but when you introduce foods to an infant, you only add one thing at a time. You don't give them anything else. It's about a 3 to 4-day period where you provide that food a few times, and then you wait and watch. You pay attention to their diaper, their skin, their mucous secretions and their attitude.

It's no different at any age in your life. If you can follow those tips and guidelines for yourself, it's amazing what you can see.

Dave: Fascinating. I feel like we could probably talk for hours, and you have so much wisdom, but we do have to wrap up this interview. If any of the readers want to connect with you or learn more about what you do, or potentially talk and get some help with their own diet, what's the best way for them to do that?

Jenn: They can go to my website, www.jennpikecom. They can also email me, jenn@jennpike.com.

Dave: Perfect. Jenn, awesome, it was so great to interview you. Thank you again for being here.

Jenn: Yeah, thank you so much for having me.

RESOURCES

Jenn's Website: http://jennpike.com

List of Hypoallergenic Foods: http://makeyourbodywork.com/hypoallergenic-foods

Understanding Food Sensitivities: http://makeyourbodywork.com/food-sensitivities

CHAPTER 6:

WHY ARE YOU EATING THAT?

In the last chapter we talked about getting off the diet rollercoaster by, in part, tracking what foods you currently eat and how your body reacts to those foods.

But have you ever wondered why you are eating those foods in the first place?

Imagine you met someone from another planet who had no concept of our eating habits here on Earth. How would you describe to them a healthy diet? What foods would you include? Which would you exclude?

I suspect you could do a really good job with this task. You know what a healthy diet looks like, but knowing something doesn't always translate into acting on that knowledge.

Serge has learned this the hard way:

> "Dave, I feel silly even writing in because I have a science degree and a background in nutrition. I could write up a perfect diet plan but I still can't seem to stick with it.
>
> I'm such an emotional eater and I snack, and snack, and snack when I'm stressed out at work. I even catch myself, but then I think I don't care and I keep eating. Do you have any tricks for people like me?"

It's often said that knowledge is power, but that's not always the case. As it is with Serge, knowledge can be useless. Knowing something doesn't help if you can't apply it to your life.

How can you take what you know about healthy eating and actually incorporate it into the food choices you make each day?

MEET SHELBY MCDANIEL

Shelby McDaniel is the owner of TNT Nutrition, an online nutrition coaching company that provides professional nutrition consulting to people all over the world. She has a degree and multiple certifications in nutrition, and is a licensed Am-I-Hungry?® Mindful Eating Facilitator which focuses heavily on food psychology.

With over 12 years in the field, she has helped thousands of people lose weight, ditch exhausting dieting, and create healthy eating habits that feel natural and effortless.

THE INTERVIEW

Dave: Hey Shelby. Thanks so much for joining me in this interview.

Shelby: Thank you for having me. I'm excited to be here.

Dave: I was reading about you on your website—TNT Nutrition—and you have an interesting designation. It says you're licensed as an *Am-I-Hungry? Licensed Mindful Eating Facilitator*. Can you tell us what that means?

Shelby: Yes. That's a special training specifically in the realm of mindful eating. The creator is a doctor. Her name is Doctor Michelle May, and she has given health professionals like ourselves the skill sets and tools we can use in our practices to help people understand more about their eating behaviors, which allows us to get to the bottom of some major issues.

She has outlined a wonderful process, which I'll be utilizing today to answer Serge's question, to look at the decision-making process surrounding why people do what they do when it comes to their eating behaviors.

You go through months of training to be able to do this. Of course, there are little checks in the boxes you have to make like with any additional training you have to complete, but the official title is the *Am-I-Hungry? Mindful Eating Facilitator*. We actually put on workshops for our clients at TNT nutrition.

Dave: That's really cool. Hearing you talk about that, it sounds very psychology-based.

Shelby: That's it in a nutshell. This is a perfect question you're giving me as an example showing it's not just about what you're eating, and I know that you know this too. If it were that easy, and it was just about proteins, and carbs, and macros, then we wouldn't be here. But it's not. It's much more in-depth.

I've been coaching for more than twelve years now, and from the beginning, I always knew it was more than that. You almost become a therapist to some people, and I've been called that. "Hey, you're a cheap therapist. I love it." I'm paying for you to be my therapist not my nutritionist." But that means I'm doing a good job. I'm asking the right questions.

Eating is intertwined with so many other areas of our life. That's why it's not so simple just to change what you're eating. It's much deeper than that, and that's what we're going to walk through today.

Dave: Yeah, you said that so well. If someone were to pool all the resources I've made, or could read certain books, or listen to podcasts, or whatever it is, and make notes of what it takes to eat a healthy diet, everyone could outline a playbook for a healthy diet. Like you said, if it were that easy, everyone would do it. But it isn't that easy.

Shelby: Yeah. I wish. And Serge—the client we're going to be addressing here today—is a perfect example, because he has a degree in nutrition. This guy knows a lot about nutrition. He can even write his own meal plans. But we will go through what's called the *Mindful Eating Cycle* with him and give him a new perspective on what's really going on here. And I think some of your readers will relate.

Dave: Yeah. That's awesome. I like that we're actually going through a process because that's practical. I want readers to walk away and know what they can do. So let's dive in, and here's a brief recap.

Serge basically says, "I know what it takes to have a healthy diet. I have a science degree. I've got a background in nutrition. I could write up my perfect diet plan, but I can't stick to it." He also mentions being stressed at work and emotional eating, so Shelby, I'll let you take it away. What are we doing here?

THE MINDFUL EATING CYCLE

Shelby: Sure. With Serge, again, he obviously knows what to eat or what he "should" be eating. That's not the issue. We need to look at why he's eating in the first place. When I work with an individual, I go through what's called the Mindful Eating Cycle. It allows me to get better insight into an individual's thinking. We start with the question "Why?"

Why am I eating?

There are actually three different cycles that we can be in at given times, and one of them is called the *Overeating Cycle*. Another is called the *Restrictive Eating Cycle*, and third is the *Instinctive Eating Cycle*.

I'm going to walk through the Mindful Eating Cycle, and I ask the same questions throughout each cycle. But the answers are all different depending on where your brain is, where you're at mentally.

With Serge, we start with why he's eating, which is the driving force to this Mindful Eating Cycle. It will then affect when he's eating and what he's eating. It will affect how he's eating, how much he's eating, and at the end, where he's investing this energy.

THE OVEREATING CYCLE AND ITS TRIGGERS

When we're talking about emotional eating, we're talking about triggers. That's a big one. When we talk about emotional eating for Serge, we're talking about stress eating. But there are so many more triggers, and I'm sure that you've heard it from your clients as well. We've got boredom eating, restless eating, we're sad, we're ticked off.

Those are emotional triggers, but we've also got environmental triggers. We see it. We're offered food. We smell it. It's in the cafeteria, right? It's free! So we've got environmental triggers and then we have physical triggers. We've got thirst. We're tired; we're fatigued. Some people eat because they're in pain. These are what we call triggers, and when someone is in the overeating cycle, like Serge, they're eating because of these triggers.

Serge has specifically said he's stressed, an emotional trigger. Then we get to the next decision-making stopping point, which is, when am I eating? When someone is in the overeating cycle, they're eating when these triggers occur. Sometimes it feels like it's all the time. If this is where you have created these habits, you're going to feel like you're in this overeating cycle all the time.

Dave: Shelby, I'm going to jump in real quick for the readers. When you were listing all those triggers, I'm sure readers put their hand up and said, "Oh yeah, that's me." And if you didn't, I'd encourage you to reread. Go back and just reread those triggers and maybe jot down which one, two, or three you think applies to you.

Shelby, as you were saying that, as soon as you said tired, my hand went up. I know when I'm tired, I feel like food will give me a burst of energy, and it's something that I can do without too much thinking. For that step, readers write down your answer to why you eat during a particular trigger. What was your why? Sorry to jump in there. Now Shelby, take us through what's our next step?

Shelby: Absolutely. Don't let me forget. We're going to go through just a couple strategies of how to meet what we call the underlying need, and I want to address yours specifically in being tired.

Dave: Done. Perfect.

Shelby: Okay, so we're going to address stress for Serge, and we're going to address yours for tiredness. This model of looking at Serge's decision-making process and how everything starts to play out starts with the big question of, "Why?"

If you're eating because of triggers—Serge is stressed, you're tired, and maybe somebody else is mad, or sad—you're not going to get a chicken salad. You're not going to get salmon and fruit. You're getting some grub. You're getting your grub on, right? You want comfort food. Again, the why—which is why we start with that question—has a direct relation to what you're eating.

If you move on to how you're eating, either because you're stressed, or again, any of those other triggers, how you're eating is usually very mindless. You're sort of in another place. We call it the autopilot zone. You're reacting to the past essentially.

If you were stressed two days ago, you're probably just doing what you always do at this point because that's the cycle you're in. So you're very mindless. You're not enjoying the meal. You're not slowing down and being mindful. You're just somewhere else.

Dave: I can relate, and a ton of the clients that I work with can relate too. We get into these patterns, and after eating a bag of chips or a bag of M&Ms or whatever it is, it's really easy to look back and think, "Holy cow, where did that just go? I don't even remember eating that."

Shelby: Well, you just led into my next stopping point which is *how much* do I eat. We're going to get into these other two cycles—the instinctive eating and the restrictive eating—here in a second. But when you're not eating to fuel your body, when it comes to how much you're eating, if and you're eating because of a trigger, how do you know when to stop?

You said it. When the bag is empty. When you're at the bottom of the pint. When the plate is scraped and licked clean. Or when the movie is over, or you're physically sick. It takes something else to tell you, "Hey, you've had enough." It's not your body wisdom. It's something else. Again, you're in this other world, and many people get into this autopilot place. It just happens. It's just on repeat constantly.

When we talk about where is he investing all of this energy, well, what do we tell clients? When you consume more fuel than what your body needs, you're consuming more energy than necessary, what happens?

Dave: We're going to gain weight.

Shelby: You're gaining weight. That's one place someone like Serge is probably investing energy when this is all said and done. He's probably also thinking, "I don't know why I keep doing this. I know this isn't good for me. What do I need to do to correct this? How much cardio do I need to do to burn this off?" He's also investing the energy mentally, maybe beating himself up, or thinking, "How can I make this better?"

What typically happens when you go your rounds on this Mindful Eating Cycle, is you want to get back on that wagon. You want to be good again. That's when people tend to head into what we call the Restrictive Eating Cycle.

THE RESTRICTIVE EATING CYCLE

This cycle is where the rules and the regulations lie. We can put almost any diet that somebody has done in the past that was a quick-fix or had some sort of crazy rules and regulations—such as taking out carbs, taking out meat entirely for two days, or fasting—in this cycle.

They're counting points rigidly, and maybe in Serge's case—and this happens a lot with people that know a lot about nutrition—the nutrition knowledge starts to build up like a rule list. I have many people that come to me with nutrition certifications. Again, just like Serge, it's not that they don't know. It just starts to become rules to them, and what do we do when we have too many rules? We want to break those rules.

Dave: Exactly. It's interesting. I like what you said when you were talking about the energy that goes into stressing out about this sort of thing because I get people that email me on a daily basis. They won't say it as clearly or simply as you just said it, but they'll talk about being in a place of seeking information. It's like they almost think if they read one more article or talk to one more expert, they're going to get the piece of information to solve their problem. That in itself becomes stressful because being in that searching mode could go on forever.

Shelby: Absolutely, so true. You're right on point. Let's keep going. You're going to understand I and see the bigger picture of how this yo-yo dieting in our society is a problem. It really is. It's not just with people who don't know about nutrition. It's happening all over.

I work with a lot of fitness and bodybuilder competitors, and these individuals do their research. They know. They're very in tune with science, but in the end, I'm consulting them to renew their relationship with food. It's the same thing with Serge from what it sounds like.

You have all of this bundled up information, and it can easily become rules. When we talk about restrictive eating, we're talking about rules and regulations. Getting back to the mindful eating cycle and going through each decision-making process, if we starting with why am I eating, we're eating because of the rules.

Serge, I think, probably goes back and forth between the overeating cycle and the rules. He goes back to eating what he's eating because it's what he feels he should be doing. In other cases, it could be another diet that somebody else is following. In Serge's case, he's just got this big buildup of information, so he's eating because of the rules.

Then we look at when somebody is eating, the next decision-making stopping point. In Serge's case—I can't speak for Serge; I'm assuming since I can't talk to him personally. I'm just going based off of my years of coaching experience on this particular subject matter. When we're looking when am I eating, for Serge, maybe he's eating because he's read a gazillion times he should be eating every three hours. That's a rule to him. For other people, maybe it's every two, or it's 9:00 pm, or it's dinner time. Even if he's not hungry, maybe he's eating because that's the rule that's in place.

Dave: I think most people probably do rule-based eating just like you just said.

Shelby: Yes, so our goal is to get out of the rule-based and get into what we call Instinctive Eating, which will be our third cycle that I'll discuss in a minute. When we move forward to "What am I eating?" when somebody is in this Restrictive Eating Cycle, such as Serge, he's eating what he feels he should be eating, what is approved. He probably understands all of the food groups.

Maybe he's got this overabundant information about macros and logging, and this is big too. I'm sure you've been exposed to people that live on things like MyFitnessPal. They're constantly logging, and it becomes like a battle zone every day to check the box, check the box, check the box. Did I get this in? Did I get this in? Did I get this in? It's like they're pressuring themselves to be good and to be a good student because it's what they feel they should be doing.

Dave: Yeah, and this entire topic of rules is interesting because for some people tracking their food like that might be good and not be stressful. They might be an analytical person who just likes to see that information. But for a lot of people, they might hear that tracking their food and watching their macros and counting calories is the way to lose weight. But for them, that actually isn't their style. Regardless, they get locked into this pattern of thinking this is the rule they heard they need to use, and therefore, they must do it. It's an awful way for them to approach it.

Shelby: Correct. You're exactly right. I have to ask people, like when I do free consultations with individuals, "Okay, what's your history? How have you tried to lose weight before?" And many of them say they log their food, but then they stop logging.

It's like this all or nothing mindset, and I'll just flat out ask them, "Hey, do you like logging?" They go, "No. I hate it." I'll say, "Well, why are you doing it?" Why are we going to continue if we hate something? Who does that? We don't do that as humans. We go away from pain and we go towards pleasure, right?

Again, this is where those rules come into play with the Restrictive Eating Cycle and what people are eating. The food logging applications can certainly play a role here. How is somebody eating when they're in this Restrictive Eating Cycle? They're eating very rigid. They're trying to be good. They're trying to check all of these boxes. Some people go as far as weighing their food. They measure their food. It's different per individual, but those are just some examples. The point is they're investing a lot of energy in this.

Dave: Yeah. It's interesting you're talking about being good versus being bad. I'm sure you see that with your clients. I see it with my clients as well. We start to label foods as good or bad. It's black and white like, and that's a dangerous place to get into. We start to develop an unhealthy relationship with food when we see certain foods as being bad, and therefore if we eat them, we are bad.

Shelby: Oh, absolutely. I think that is a huge underlying problem Serge may be experiencing here just because of what he knows from his nutrition background.

Nutrition almost becomes a weapon rather than a tool for many people. So the next stopping point is how much am I eating then. And getting back to trackers, getting back to rigid meal plans, or other sorts of diet programs, how much is already predetermined?

You're given a certain amount of carbs per day, or calories, or percentages, or just what's on your meal plan. There is absolutely no affiliation or connection to feeling full, feeling content, determining how much we should be eating.

Again, I don't know how much energy Serge is specifically investing, but when we're in this restrictive eating cycle, it's pretty obvious. We're investing a ton of energy thinking about food, weight, weight-loss, did I get all this done, or do I have everything with me? It's overwhelming, right?

THE PENDULUM ANALOGY

We'll use an analogy. We're going to use an analogy of a pendulum, a pendulum that swings right to left. If we were to swing this pendulum to the right—and the right direction means the Restrictive Eating Cycle—it's like we're trying to hold this pendulum all the way to the right.

We're trying to control all these variables so we can be good and do what we "should be doing." What's going to happen? At some point, eventually, you're just going to let go and say, "Screw it." It's way too much to sustain to try to be perfect. The striving for perfection today, when it comes to our eating, is out of this world. People panic over the smallest things. So if you're trying to be a perfectionist, you need to find another way because it isn't going to happen.

Dave: Particularly too, when we're trying to eat to perfection on someone else's rules it's very hard to do because we don't have buy-in. We weren't part of the process of creating those rules. It was something that maybe we read or someone else dictated to us. It's very hard to maintain that for any meaningful length of time.

Shelby: Absolutely, and that is what we're up against. It's hard to ask someone, "Hey, just forget everything that you've been exposed to."

You can't do that. So this is how I can, over time, get through to an individual and help them to separate emotionally from these rules, and just bring awareness to their eating, so they understand why they're doing what they're doing. Going through these three cycles gives them a better idea of how they're maybe in the Restrictive Eating Cycle, Overeating Cycle, and the goal is to be in the Instinctive

Eating Cycle. Serge question's, as simple as it may sound, is not so simple to answer.

There are many levels to it. That's why today I'm doing my best to give as much information as I can, but it goes deeper than what he's giving me regarding the question and the problem.

Once somebody lets go of that pendulum—getting back to this pendulum swing—they go right into this Overeating Cycle. We're talking about triggers. What trigger forces individuals to let go of this pendulum? It's deprivation. It's restriction. That is the number one emotional trigger. We're eating because of triggers.

We're eating when those triggers occur. We're eating comfort foods. We're eating fats. We're eating mindlessly. We're not stopping when we're full, and now we're guilty. And what do we do? Boom. We go right back to the rules and the regulations. The solution in many people's eyes—another diet program, more rules, and regulations—is actually the problem.

Dave: What is the solution? How does someone make the jump from being in that pendulum and swinging back and forth into instinctive eating?

Shelby: We have to relearn our body wisdom. We have to go back to our innate ability to determine when we're hungry, what we need to eat, how much we need to eat, etc. We're all born with this. Think about it. What do babies do when they're hungry?

Dave: Yeah, they cry.

Shelby: They cried. No one's saying, "Hey baby. It's three hours. Why aren't you eating yet?" No. They cry. Their body knows. When a baby gets enough food what do they do?

Dave: Yeah, they stop. This is so interesting you bring this up. I was just visiting my sister, and she has two young children. At dinner—there's a two-year-old and a five-year-old—both of them just stopped eating and didn't want to finish their meal, and they liked their meal. I remember thinking, "Wow, I'll eat that for you."

Shelby: Exactly.

Dave: For kids, yeah, they eat just as much as they need to eat.

Shelby: Kids are the best forms of examples of instinctive eating because they haven't been exposed to all of these rules and regulations in our food abundant society yet. And it's not just the rules. There's food everywhere around us.

That's the goal, to get back to the instinctive eating characteristics. So we're going back through the mindful eating cycle and looking at what the answers will be when someone learns to trust their bodies again.

The tracking and all the rules take away from our ability to tune into what we want and need. We're too busy, and we're too distracted trying to please everyone and everything else, and we just lose ourselves in the process.

Once again, let's picture this pendulum swing. We don't want to be all the way to the right where we're holding this pendulum. We also don't want to be all the way to the left in this overeating cycle, in this autopilot and very negative place.

We want to be somewhere softly in between the pendulum swing, where it's more neutral. It's softly swaying a little to the right. It's softly swaying a little to the left, but it's not in either cycle. It's very calm.

THE INSTINCTIVE EATING CYCLE

Dave: What is the reason for eating when someone gets to that neutral place?

Shelby: When someone is instinctively eating, why are they eating?

Dave: Ideally, it's because physiologically they need food.

Shelby: Exactly. They're fueling their bodies. It's a saying out there, eat to fuel your body, but most people really do not understand what that feels like and what the body needs. It's good in theory, but they've never personally experienced it.

Now, there are some individuals out there who showcase a lot of instinctive eating habits, and it's hard for them to understand why some people just can't stop eating. They're not there. They're not in those other cycles very often. They are very blessed and fortunate to keep their instinctive abilities.

When the goal is to get into this Instinctive Eating Cycle, people are eating to fuel their bodies. So when does somebody eat when they're in this Instinctive Eating Cycle? When they're hungry, just like the baby, right? They eat when they're hungry.

The problem with this is over time, people try to eat based on everybody else's rules or because of triggers. I have worked with individuals who are nervous they can't tell when they're physically hungry anymore, and it's a huge relearning process.

For others, it's much easier. They feel that little rumble in their stomach or they're losing focus and losing energy. And that is what they are tuning in to determine when they need to eat. These signs from their stomach and from their glucose levels say, "Hey, my fuel gauge is starting to go on E here. I need to eat."

Dave: Even that idea of understanding what it feels like to be hungry is something that's lost. You talked about how plentiful food is in our society, and it's so true. I'd say most of us very rarely experience true hunger.

Shelby: Agreed. And many people have experienced a couple of situations with hunger. They might have had a bad experience where they got so hungry, and something bad happened. Maybe they passed out, or they got sick, something really terrible. So their mission becomes never to get hungry again. They do what's called *passive eating*, and they just eat by the clock. Can't get hungry. Can't get hungry. Can't get hungry. And once again, we're moving away from our body wisdom.

It's a little scary sometimes for people to feel a little hungry. It's a fear for many people, and for some people, they kind of cruise through this one. They realize, "Hey, I'm in tune with my hunger cues, which is great, so I don't have to spend a ton of time in this particular area." Everyone's a little different here.

EATING FOR NOURISHMENT OR PLEASURE?

When it comes to what somebody is eating in the Instinctive Eating Cycle, this is where it gets interesting. We look at what we need to nourish our bodies, but it's not just about nourishing our bodies physically.

We have what's called *two worlds*. One is eating for nourishment, which is when we're trying to be "good" and give our bodies everything that it needs to flourish and to thrive. Proteins, calories, and things for medical purposes that work for us. Maybe somebody doesn't feel well on dairy, or grains, which are reasons why people choose specific foods for their diet.

Now, that is eating for nourishment, but the world everyone misses is this world of eating for pleasure. We think this is a forbidden world. This is also a world where rules in the past—perhaps in Serge's world for example—label foods as bad. We are human, and we have to learn how to allow these two worlds to coexist and overlap slightly. How much they overlap is different per individual, but we have needs as humans for moderation.

We have needs for interest. We have needs for variety, which is found in the world of eating for pleasure. We tend to ignore those needs, and when we ignore them, that's when we go from restrictive eating to overeating and vice versa. We just have to let these two worlds exist.

When you take the restrictions off and say, "Nothing is off limits," that's very scary for people. They think, "I'm going to eat everything and gain all this weight." But this process is so amazing when you just learn to trust it. It changes everything so dynamically.

When you give yourself permission, the power food—or certain foods—has over you starts to dissipate because you're tuned in now to what you really want. You'll decide maybe you just want a couple of bites, or you think, "I'm actually good. I'll pass." This happens when you're not pressured to make a life or death decision to eat something you feel is bad.

Dave: The end of Serge's comment says, "Do you have any tricks for people like me." So for someone who's trying to make mindful decisions about what they're eating, and they're trying to be in tune with their body—practically speaking—what can they start to do to develop that strategy?

STRATEGIES FOR MORE MINDFUL EATING

Number one, he needs to ask himself, "Am I even hungry?" It sounds like he already knows the answer to this question, which is good. Some people don't, and they're just habitually eating, and they don't even know they're doing it. This question allows people to put on the brakes for a second and say "Whoa, all right, what's going on here?"

For Serge, if he knows he's not hungry, he's not in this Instinctive Eating Cycle, he's not trying to fuel his body, he has triggers giving him this urge to eat. What can we do? We've got a couple of options here. One, not necessarily in Serge's case, but in general, if somebody has an urge to eat and they know they're not hungry, how do they get around it?

They can eat anyway—which you may find surprising I'm saying that, but think about this scenario.

Okay, somebody has an office party, and its Bob's going away party. Everyone is collaborating, and they're spending time together, final moments with Bob, and they're passing out cake. You may decide it's a need for you to meet to enjoy this camaraderie with your team. Maybe you haven't had cake in a while. That is not a mindless choice.

You're looking at the needs that you're meeting by eating this cake, so it is a choice. You can eat. If you continuously eat when you're not hungry, then yeah, it can become a problem, but just because you choose to eat something when you're not hungry doesn't mean you're necessarily mindless. That's part of normal eating. It's when it becomes excessive, where it becomes problematic.

Dave: Sorry to jump in here, but focusing on your language, the idea of "choice." I think that's really important for the readers. Think about the office party example. I know that happens to people at times. Someone brings in cookies or whatever it is, cake. The choice, stopping for a few seconds and deciding if you're going to have whatever portion size of this, that is a mindful choice. You say you feel okay with this, and it's not going to turn into three or four or five servings of whatever the food is.

107

Shelby: Exactly. Mindful eating doesn't necessarily mean it doesn't relate to nutrient-dense choices. It's just being aware of your choices. That's all that it is. You're in the moment. That's option one.

Option two, he can do what most people have heard before, redirect his attention. He's stressed. He sees the cookies on Jody's desk, and he says, "Okay, I know this. I'm just stressed out. I'm going to go and sidetrack myself." That is an option, but the best option for Serge and anyone else, you have to deal with the underlying need at hand.

If it is stress, then for Serge, he needs to say "Okay, do I need some more down time? Am I not giving myself five minutes a day to just take a breath? Do I need to turn the radio down on the way home to just relax my brain a little bit? Do I need an earlier bedtime? Do I need to socialize a little bit more? Do I need to go to church more?" There are so many things as far as an underlying need that can help him deal with this stress.

Dave: I love the fact that you mentioned a bunch of ideas that aren't food related. Quite often the solution becomes, "Okay, I'm not going to eat cookies, and I will replace it with fruit or whatever it is." But some things satisfy these psychological needs—and perhaps physiological needs as well—that aren't even food.

Shelby: Absolutely. Normally, when it's an emotional need, it's not about food at all. Maybe somebody is mad; they need to have a conversation with somebody, they need to jot down their thoughts, or whatever it is. You need to address your needs and wants. When you address the need, the food will just poof. It'll be gone. You won't even think of it.

You're going to feel so much better after you meet this need. And the next time this situation rolls around, you realize, "Okay, I need to meet this need again." You will want to go toward meeting the underlying need versus food because it felt awesome.

Dave: Yeah. It's such a win.

Shelby: Yes. It's such a win. Food? Forget it. It won't be your go to anymore. You just kicked it to the curb.

USING "IF-THEN" STATEMENTS

Dave: Shelby, as you were talking, you just reminded me of an article I recently read that was talking about something called *if-then statements*. The strategy is you think about areas in your life where you're susceptible to temptations. Since we're talking about food, I'll use Serge's example.

The *if* portion would be, "If I'm feeling stressed at work," and the typical response might be, "I eat cookies." Instead, Serge comes up with this if-then statement: "If I'm feeling stressed at work, *then* I will go for a walk," or, "then I will call my friend," or, "then I will..." And think of whatever that *then* statement can be for you. Then you have this construct in your mind, and it doesn't have to be this huge ordeal when that if statement happens because you've already created it before it even happens.

Shelby: Agreed, and you said the keyword, "before" it happens. In the minds of my clients, they have built up these situations to be this huge ordeal, but I give them assignments to figure out the solution in five minutes or less. I'll tell people, "Look. Take five minutes. That's all."

You're worth five minutes a week. Just stop and think, "Hey, what are other things that I can do to meet this underlying need?" Boom. They'll just list, list, and list. Now they have all of these options when that time rolls around, and when that autopilot wiring of the brain wants to take place and eat instead, guess what? Now they have all these other options, and they're on their way to creating new habits.

They're not going to be an ace-in-the-hole every single time. I wish it were that easy, but it's going to get a lot easier the more practice you put in, and that's the key. Again, you can't expect perfection. These are habits.

When you're eating emotionally, these are habits that have been with you probably for some time. So give yourself a little break, a little breathing room, to practice and don't beat yourself up if the autopilot behavior sometimes wins one minor battle. You're going to have a lot more battles. In the end, you're going to win the war.

Dave: Now Shelby, before we end, I know a lot of readers probably have questions about this process or maybe questions about their own situation. Where can they connect with you if they want to find out more?

Shelby: Sure. Well, you can sign up for a free consultation. If you want a little bit more information, just go to TNTnutrition.org. It has a big red symbol in the corner to book a free consult. You can also get involved with our blog. We do a lot of blogging, as you do, specifically in the mindful eating department and other areas too. But we've got a lot of great articles and resources already online that are available.

We're providing some free downloads as well, so that's a great way to keep up with us. That's where I would say to check out the information.

Dave: I appreciate that. For the readers, if you go to the *Resources* section at the end of this chapter, I'll have a link to Shelby's website and also to her mindful eating download. Maybe, Shelby, you can just tell us quickly, what will people get when they download that?

Shelby: Sure. It's a free video download which will to be a nice little recap of what we talked about today, getting to the bottom of fundamental struggles people have with their eating.

Dave: Shelby, thanks again for being here. You're an awesome guest, and thanks for all the advice you've given.

Shelby: Hey, no problem. Thanks for having me. I appreciate it, Dave.

RESOURCES

Shelby's Website: http://www.tntnutrition.org

Shelby's Mindful Eating Download: http://makeyourbodywork.com/shelby-mindful-eating

CHAPTER 7:

ARE YOU ADDICTED TO SUGAR?

Are you an addict?

The word "addiction" often conjures up thoughts of drug or alcohol dependency, but the most common addiction we face today is to food. Particularly powerful is sugar addiction.

No matter how hard you try to resist, a sugar addiction will always outlast your willpower. Battling sugar cravings with good intentions and sheer determination is a losing cause. There must be an easier way to overcome sugar addiction, right?

Susan asked this very question:

> *"Sometimes I like to eat junk. If I can just eat what I know I should eat, I'm fine. I totally know what is good and what to avoid in my head, but when I get tempted, or when I get down, or when I'm happy, or whenever, I put in a little sugar and then I'm hooked on sugar all day, or all week, or all whatever, until I can say no completely again.*
>
> *I love to exercise, there's no problem there, but what can I do about this sugar addiction?"*

Breaking your sugar addiction will take more than effort and stronger willpower. Jennifer Powter explains how you can do it once and for all.

MEET JENNIFER POWTER

 Jennifer Powter conquered her own struggles with weight by finding the right life balance and the right approach to eating and exercise.

She now coaches other women from around the world who are looking to achieve the same goal. Jennifer has her MSc. in Exercise Physiology, is a certified Exercise Physiologist and EQ consultant, and is also a Professional Co-Active Coach.

THE INTERVIEW

Dave: Hey, Jennifer, thanks so much for joining me in this interview today.

Jennifer: Hey. Thank you. I'm so happy to be here.

Dave: You have an interesting story. I know you own your own company and you've got two kids. You sound like someone who's so busy, but yet, you have quite a story of health, progress, and success. Maybe you can start off by sharing, where did you come from? What have you achieved?

Jennifer: Thank you, I will. Sometimes when you hear somebody is in the fitness industry, people immediately think, "Oh, well, it's probably easy for her," or, "It's so easy for him." I really would like readers to know, it wasn't long ago I found myself carrying 35 extra pounds after I had my kids.

It was just such a strange thing to experience because my degree is in this field. I've got a master's in Exercise Physiology, I've done Iron Man, and I've run so many marathons. Yet, there I was, night after night eating chocolate chips and drinking wine. I wasn't taking great care of myself.

About a year and a half later I was like, "God, why can't I lost this baby weight?" I thought I needed to exercise more. I was already tired and sleep deprived with kids, but I registered for a race and immersed myself into a pretty rigorous training regime. I just burned out.

I had to go back to the research and take a look at—for myself—how do I manage all of the busy aspects of my life and still take care of myself? I'm happy to say, I did figure it out.

Obviously, it took some time and some effort, but I got back to the weight I felt good at, and I enjoyed wearing my clothes again. Now, I help other women do or follow the same path. It is possible, that's the great thing. It is possible.

Dave: I love that message. Can you say it again? That it doesn't mean you have to exercise way more?

Jennifer: Yeah. Knowing the industry, the most common thing I hear is, "Oh, I just don't have time to exercise," or, "I'm so busy already, I can't exercise."

What I say all the time is, "Exercise is wonderful, but at the end of the day, we simply cannot out train our nutrition." What we put into our bodies matters. It matters more than we even realize. The peak of my awareness was when I started to get a real understanding of food and its impact.

Dave: That's a nice segue into Susan's question today. I know you read Susan's question, but to recap, she says she knows what to eat but then falls down the same path. She'll eat a little bit of sugar. She specifically mentions sugar a couple of times and says it spirals out of control. Is that something you see a lot? Do you work with clients who are in the same boat?

Jennifer: Yeah, I do. I'll hear people self-described as sugar addicts, or carb-aholics, or having a sweet tooth. They can't figure it out, and they try to do all of these extreme things like detox to eliminate it entirely. I focus on the food. I tell clients, "That craving is attempting to numb some sort of emotion you're not willing to face or to feel."

Food has become so confusing in our world. We think we should eat good and if we eat something bad, we're bad. We compartmentalize our emotional self from our physical self. Yet, they're so linked.

WHY WE ALL CRAVE SUGAR

Dave: Okay, that's interesting. I'd like you to dive deeper. Can you talk about cravings and what part of a craving is physiological versus psychological or emotional?

Jennifer: Yeah. Both are at play. Such a brilliant question! If you're reading this, you have to understand your cravings are comprised of 2 things. It's exactly what Dave said. There is a physiological component because sugar acts on your brain. Sugar has this direct pathway to your brain where it stimulates the part of your brain that secretes feel good hormones and neurotransmitters that say, "Yes, this makes me feel so awesome."

Once you feel that way, you want to feel it more. But your mouth and taste buds respond to the flavor, or the sensation, of sweetness. The more sweet or sugar you have, the more you want.

I always say, "You never crave the change you're creating. You crave what you've always done." You have to give yourself enough time to adapt and adjust to cutting back on sugar, while simultaneously working on the emotional, psychological aspect of what you're using the sugar for.

Dave: I could not agree more. The trouble with that answer is it seems hard to approach. I'm just imagining what the readers' are thinking right now. "Okay, so I get it, there's this physiological component where my body does want the effect, that stimulant sugar gives us. But it's hard to break those habits and patterns ingrained in our life." Can you start with one or the other and talk about, what do you do? How do you deal with that?

WHAT DO YOUR FOOD HABITS REALLY LOOK LIKE?

Jennifer: When I work with my clients, we always start with the practical, like, "Why am I doing what I'm doing? What am I doing? The Mocha Frappuccino and the lemon loaf I might grab at Starbucks, what is that physiologically doing to me?" So often, we become unconscious about our habits around food.

We might drive to Starbucks, hop out, grab a coffee, throw in some cream, dump a cup of sugar packets in it. It's what we do now. We lack the consciousness and awareness of what we're putting into our body.

We cannot change what we're not aware of. The first step is awareness. What are you eating? Then, write it down. So often people resist writing it down, and yet when my clients do it, they're very often shocked at the end of the week of all the crap going into their body.

When they're doing it in spurts throughout the week, the handfuls, the little bag here, the grabbing of the handful there, it just doesn't seem like much until you add it up. That's the first piece.

Dave: When you start writing it down, it's not always going to be an immediate reaction. We talk about food sensitivities versus a full-blown reaction, like an allergy, which we might have to a food. You might eat something and then manifest into symptoms 8 hours later. It really does take some consciousness. Like you said, using the word consciousness, start to identify some of those links.

Jennifer: I went to a lecture Dave, and I wish I could remember who spoke. I'm going to ask you a personal question, have you ever been hungover? From alcohol?

Dave: Years ago, it was a long time.

Jennifer: Me too, it's been forever, but I certainly have been. What he said is most of us are walking around with food hangovers every single day, but it's become our new normal. We actually have no idea what good health and energy is available to us because of our day to day habits. We just think, how we feel is the way we feel, and it's normal. I thought that was so interesting. I began to see and experiment in my own life, and it was actually quite true.

PHYSIOLOGICAL VERSUS EMOTIONAL HUNGER

Dave: That is interesting. With the clients you work with, how do you help them? Because those reactions or those symptoms aren't necessarily directly tied time-wise to the foods you eat. How do you help someone chart that out and record it?

Jennifer: I work specifically with helping women who have tried everything to lose weight and can't, but still really want to. They have a bit of hope left. I approach from a very scientific nature, and then we dive into the emotional part. It's about paying attention to when you feel the resistance.

When you know you shouldn't do something, and you do it anyways, I always ask what else is going on in your life at that time? There's going to be a trigger for why you want what you want, and you might not even know it. The trigger could be a time of day. Maybe it's 3:00 and all your co-workers are getting up to go for a walk to the local bakery.

Maybe it's people you're around. Your boss stresses you out and every time you have a meeting you want to eat chocolate. Maybe it's at night. Between 8:00 and 11:00 are very tough times for my clients, and they feel like having something to eat.

I really help my clients distinguish between true physiological hunger and emotional hunger. Not many people understand what we're emotionally hungry for. Often, we have to develop that awareness.

Dave: It's interesting because—you've probably heard this as well—sometimes I'll work with clients and they'll say, at a certain time of day, "I just really need –" The idea of *needing* is more of a psychological thing. We feel like we really want it or it makes us feel good, or it helps in a situation, but does our body need it?

Jennifer: It helps us get through sometimes. I think it's both. A lot of my clients are protein deficient, so they either grab a coffee in the morning, don't have breakfast, running on empty until lunch, and eat a salad because they're trying to be good. There's just not a lot of good energy coming so, of course, they feel crappy by 3:00 or 4:00.

They've just gone through their whole day with almost nothing to fuel them, so they crave quick energy. In many ways, their brain is sending them a signal, "Eat something. I'm crashing here." They do. They go out and grab something sugary, and they get a sugar rush. Then they're thinking, "Okay, now I can power through the next few hours." Whether it's the tedious tasks of work or the chauffeuring of kids to all sorts of activities.

DISCOVERING YOUR UNIQUE SOLUTION

Dave: I want to get back to the idea of tying our symptomatology to the foods that we eat. But first, I have a really cool story. I got an email this week.

Her story was so encouraging. She said, "I eat almonds, that's my go-to snack. After listening to your podcast, I realized that after I eat the almonds, within an hour or 2 my body felt…" and her term was, "yuck." She just said, "I just felt yuck, and I never put those two and two together." Since it was a short window of time after the symptoms appeared, it's quite easy to identify the link.

What would you say to someone who has symptoms 8 hours later or the next day, or that night and it's harder to pinpoint what caused the problem?

Jennifer: Yeah. That's a great question. I think, to be honest, so many times when you ask the question, I find it easier when you have to answer the question to somebody else. When I was alone in my struggle on my journey, I knew red wine and chocolate chips between 8 and 10 at night probably were not my best choices. I'm hoping somebody else can relate.

Dave: Don't you worry, all the hands are going up right now, I know.

Jennifer: Yeah, I was really in denial. I can look back now and clearly see I was in such denial about what was happening in my life. I didn't have anyone to process or talk it through with. Often, we don't want to change the way we're living until it starts to feel so bad, change seems better than continuing on as we are.

Maybe it's when your pants feel too tight, or you feel too gross in your gut, or you have headaches that don't go away. I don't think I'm totally answering your question, but at some point, you have an inner knowing that what you're doing is not taking you down a good path.

Most of my clients say they know they're not doing what they should be but can't seem to stop. That's the first indication there are some emotions at play. Maybe it's job stress, relationship stress, or you're just not getting enough sleep.

So many of my clients go, go, go all day and then between 9 and 11 feel like they've got "me time." So they stay awake, maybe watching something, or catching up on Facebook. They really just need to go to bed.

To learn true self-care, I had to go back to the basics. I had to re-parent myself in a way, which is kind of a broad term, but I had to learn how to take care of myself. I used to wish for a fairy godmother of health to come into my life and just do it for me. It was ultimately real accountability and sense of personal responsibility to stop feeling so crappy.

WHAT ARE YOU WILLING TO GIVE UP?

Dave: Something really wise you eluded to was the idea of taking a look at what we want to change and then figuring out what we are willing to give up to achieve change? I'll use your example of watching Netflix or checking out Facebook at night.

Say you want to lose weight, and you're chronically fatigued, but you get comfort, enjoyment, and community from going on Facebook. If giving that up is actually more of a sacrifice than being 10 or 15 pounds overweight, then maybe it's okay to do those things. What do you think about that?

Jennifer: I think that's okay. It becomes a personal choice. It becomes a conscious choice. It becomes saying, "I'm going to do this and therefore I'm willing not to have that." What I find happens is most people don't make a conscious choice, and it becomes, "I'm a failure, I can't get that, so I'm just going to do this." It's like second place in a way.

It's like they don't believe that what they really want can happen, or it's going to be too hard for them, or they tried in the past and they failed. Perhaps the failure has a bitter taste preventing them from trying again. I find there's a lot of fear people need to push through because I truly think a lot of people want it but are scared of what it might take to get it. But once they get it, it's so worth it.

There's resistance we have to be willing to push through, which is why often, most of us need support. I make no hesitation in saying to people I am a certified personal trainer and I still reached out and hired my own trainer. I am a coach, I reached out, and I got help because I could not do it on my own. For some reason, there's a belief we should be able to do this on our own.

Dave: I 100% agree. Going back to something you said at the start of this interview, you talked about working with women who have tried everything and still aren't able to lose weight. I don't mean to be insensitive, but the idea of trying everything, that's a very subjective term, and someone could say, "Well, I've tried everything."

In reality, when you boil it down, "Oh, I tried everything without giving up this, and without sacrificing that, and well, I can't change that because." I'm not just speaking for our clients, it's for me too. I do that all the time: "I wish I could be like that but I can't because of this." It becomes this inner dialog, "Well, what am I willing to give up? What am I willing to change? How much do I want it?"

THE SURE PATH TO WEIGHT-LOSS

Jennifer: Absolutely. I think you and I might be on the same page, but I'm not going to speak for you. You can agree or disagree, but so many solutions in our industry are short-term, quick-fix solutions. Two weeks of this, 30 days of that, 10 pounds in 10 days, build muscle.

We see all these fitspo pictures on Instagram, Facebook, Pinterest. But we don't understand the weight-gain took time or that genuine weight-loss and health transformation also takes time. I'll usually make an analogy around money, it's like you want to make or save a million dollars, but you're spending everything you make every single day.

You're constantly frustrated you don't have a million dollars in the bank. You can see why. It's because you're spending it everywhere all the time. If you really want the million dollars, you have to cut back on your spending and save it.

With money, it's such a tangible thing, it makes sense. With weight-loss, food, health, and fitness, these things are more confusing for people because it requires energy, time, and some confidence. Some lifestyle habits get slippery when you are busy with a career, kids, and work-life pressures.

Dave: I agree. I love that analogy. The unfortunate thing with money is it's a linear path. If I save this many dollars per day, I will have this much at the end of the day, whereas it is a little more ambiguous with weight-loss because everyone's different and the path isn't direct.

Jennifer: Yeah. It can be. I think that there can be a direct path, but it's a slower path. A lot of women think they should consistently be able to lose 5 pounds week after week after week. It's just simply not physiologically possible. Of course, it depends on where you start, but that's a lot of pure fat loss.

That's very much beyond a healthy physiological expectation. Often what we think should happen versus what we're doing—which is actually successful—don't match up. This is why it's so important to find great advice or guidance.

Dave: That's an inspirational message. Readers, if you take away one thing, it should be what Jen just said. The idea of perpetually losing weight and continuing to do so forever, even if you've heard or met someone who has done that, doesn't mean it's going to happen for me, for you, or for anyone else.

Jennifer: I have some clients who lose a pound a week or a pound-and-a-half. After a month, if 5 or 6 pounds are shed, I am double high-fiving and fist-pumping because that's amazing. In 6 months, if you keep it up, 30 pounds are gone, and if you lifted a 30-pound dumbbell lately, that's a lot of weight.

Dave: Agreed.

SILENCING YOUR INNER CRITIC

Jennifer: For me, I remember picking up weights in the gym after I lost weight on my body and thinking, "God, no wonder I was so tired all the time." It took me over 8 months of consistent focus, and some weeks I didn't lose any.

Again, I do not live in a world of only eating algae and spinach. Sometimes people think you have to be extreme. I've got kids, we eat cake, and we bake, and we do stuff, and I still enjoy wine. But I did enough emotional work to ensure food was not a coping mechanism.

Dave: That idea of building a proper relationship with food—I know that sounds cliché—is true. It's a relationship.

Jennifer: Yeah. I think we fail to recognize we're in relationships with our kids, partners, friends, and ourselves. But there's a little mean voice—I know some of you readers know what I'm talking about—that says the meanest things to you, things you would never say to anybody else.

You're in that relationship every single day. We have to learn how to cultivate a healthier, more positive, happier relationship with ourselves. One not so full of shame, blame, and guilt.

Dave: Yeah, I couldn't agree more. Okay, this is an embarrassing story, but a friend of mine got me hooked on a TV show called The Mindy Project.

Jennifer: Oh, yeah.

Dave: I don't know, whatever, it's a great show. It's really funny. The season I'm in right now, Mindy is pregnant, and is having a disparaging conversation with herself talking about how she's fat, how she's ugly, and how could anyone love her. It's the same sort of thing. No one would ever say that to someone else, but it seems like we get this free pass to be our own worst critic all the time.

Jennifer: Yeah. I literally call it the inner critic. Sometimes I use a bit more profanity when I describe the little voice inside, I won't in this interview. So many people have become accustomed to listening to the voice they've got inside, it becomes who they are. That's part of the work.

As an Emotional Intelligence Practitioner, that is part of the blend I bring to the physiology and science of weight-loss. How do we work to calm down this part of ourselves and not let it be the driver of our life?

CELEBRATE EVERY LITTLE VICTORY

It's amazing, and that's why change is possible. But you have to understand the process of change and how human you are, how normal it is to face bumps and roadblocks. It does not imply failure, it just means plot twist. You've got to move through this.

Sometimes I think if we really want something, it should be easy for us, and in my experience, this isn't the case. We can really want something, but there are still going to be challenges and little forks, deviations in the road to getting there. This is how we learn.

Dave: I totally agree. The idea of embracing our wins. This week, in one of the programs I run—it's called the *10 in 4 Challenge*—there was a participant who had lost about 13 pounds in the first 3 weeks.

Everyone was cheering, and it was really exciting for her, but then I saw a comment from another woman. She said, "I only lost 2 pounds this week." It's like you were saying—double high-fives—everyone should be so excited. I said to her, "Embrace the win because a week ago, you were still carrying those 2 pounds and I know compared to someone who lost 13 pounds it might seem small, but that is a win."

Jennifer: Yeah. It totally is. My market is mostly women, it's who I work with. One of the things I do in a group program I lead is every single call we start it off with, "Tell me the new, the good, and what are you celebrating?" We have these accomplishments, but we'll just jump from one to the other without even giving pause to recognizing where we're kicking some butt in life.

Instead, we'll be like, "I'm not doing this, I didn't do this well." I focus on saying my accomplishment and sharing it. And then I feel proud of it so I can build up the muscle of confidence. I agree, celebrating our little wins along the way has got to be a part of the process.

Dave: It replaces that negative dialog we can have with ourselves. I know I'll stop in the day and think, "Hey Dave, you're really good at this." It does feel good. Some of those self-doubts or other things I don't like about myself are then less potent.

ATTUNE TO THE POSITIVE

Jennifer: Yeah. I've got a personal story if you have time.

Dave: Yeah.

Jennifer: Great. I have a son who's 8, and my daughter is 6. She was upset last night about something, and I was downstairs, hearing them talk. She was like, "I'm a dummy, I'm an idiot." I heard my son say, "Liv, don't think those things. If you think those things, you're going to feel really badly about yourself and they're not true anyway."

Never have I been more proud of my kids. She's like, "Yeah, I guess." He says, "Tell me all the ways you are smart Liv." He's 8. It was such a beautiful moment to be privy to but not involved in. That night, going to bed, I said, "Jake, how did you know that?" He's like, "Well, I hear you talk about all the time Mom."

Those are some of the things I say. Think the good, choose the good. The choice is ours. What do we want to see in the world? It does take practice because we're very much attuned to the negative. I think it's just such a cool thing to remember: the choice is ours. We're doing great, or we suck. Which one makes you feel better to think? I feel better if I think, "Yeah, I'm doing great, lots to learn, but I'm still doing great."

Dave: I love that story, it's so heart-warming to hear you say that. Wow, congratulations. Honestly, congratulations on good parenting.

Jennifer: There are lots of fails, trust me. There are lots of fails in my life. At that moment, I'm like, "You are learning all of the things you need to know, you two are amazing." Anybody who has kids out there, my kids can love each other until they want to kill each other sometimes. At that moment it was so tender, and I thought, "What if we can be that tender with ourselves?"

Dave: Now, I know, I feel like you and I, we're having a little pep rally here just talking mindset and all these different shifts as we work towards change. Getting back to Susan's question, where she's talking about sugar, and we addressed a lot of that.

Let's talk about that action step. What would you say? Where could Susan, or anyone who's like her, start today to beat their sugar addiction?

Jennifer: Yeah, I'd love to share that. It's funny that we've gotten acquainted with each other because I've become super passionate about shedding light on the role of sugar in our lives. Part of it has stemmed from my own research, and really how the food industry has played a huge role in our sugar consumption.

I've become so passionate about it, writing blog posts, creating content around it. I think that if you really want to know more, come and check out a blog post that I wrote called *Is Sugar Really so Bad?*

That's the name of it, but you can also go to www.jenniferpowter.com/quicksugarswaps, where you can get access to this e-book I've created, which is about the top 7 seemingly innocent foods that you should probably avoid if you want to decrease your sugar consumption, and what you can eat instead.

What I find so frustrating is people will often tell you what you shouldn't do, what you can't have, and then you're left with no alternative. It's like, "Don't eat this, don't have that."

I really wanted to make this easy for people in my community and anybody else who can get their hands on it, to know some real simple things you can do with products you're bringing into your house, that you can still enjoy but in a slightly different way. It will have a huge impact on your sugar consumption.

Dave: It's really hard to say, "I'm going from being a sugar addict to saying, cold turkey, I'm not going to eat sugar anymore." That idea, I love that you put that resource together, that idea of swapping out some of the worst offenders and then having something as an alternative. That's fantastic.

Jennifer: Yeah. Can I share a quick one with you right now?

Dave: Yeah, please.

Jennifer: Okay. This is the one that, for most of my clients and my aunts, even my friends. Many people buy yogurt, we think yogurt's a health food. But, for a lot of my clients, they're buying yogurt that's a flavoured yogurt or a fruit based yogurt, so raspberry, strawberry, or coconut, or lemon.

What's so crazy is when you're eating that yogurt, you literally are taking in as much sugar as if you are eating a candy bar, or chocolate bar. Yet, we think we're being healthy with it, right? People are like, "Oh, gross, but I hate the taste of plain yogurt."

An easy swap right now is go half and half, get that plain yogurt into your house and then buy the flavoured yogurt, but do 50%, 50%, or half a cup of plain and a quarter cup of the flavoured.

What's amazing is as you play with the ratios, eventually you will reach a point where even a tablespoon of the flavoured stuff added to your plain yogurt will be enough. I can say that because I had to rehab myself with yogurt. Once I learned about it, I'm like, "Oh my God, I'm giving this to my kids in their lunches." Anyways, I've got lots of very practical tips like that in that resource, because again, you might not know.

Dave: That's a great one. I remember I used to eat, do you know what fruit bottom yogurt is?

Jennifer: Yeah, totally.

Dave: I remember just thinking it was absolutely delicious. Again, I'm embarrassed to say this but I would eat all the yogurt and then just have the fruit at the bottom and then eat the fruit. It's like eating super sugar jam or something. Now the idea, just after having gotten away from that type of food, I imagine eating that would probably be pretty gross.

Jennifer: That's exactly it because your taste buds have changed. I talk a lot about this. Food companies have optimized food to help you reach a bliss point, that's what they call it, mathematicians and food scientists.

What's crazy, for any of you moms who are reading, your kids have a bliss point that is twice as high as an adults, which is why when they're eating stuff and you're like, "Oh my God, how can you stand that? It's so sweet." We're really conditioning them to handle sweet and want even more.

Again, from that brain chemistry and the physiology of sensory taste receptors, yeah, for me both, if I put coffee in my sugar now it's like, "Ew, disgusting."

At one point I couldn't have imagined giving it up. I think that, again, it's like inspiration, right? You and I are both in this industry and yet we've both done things and we've looked back like, "Oh, I don't know how I could've done that." When you do it, you can't imagine not doing it. It is possible.

Dave: Just so wise and I love the idea of just doing it step by step. Readers out there who are yogurt eaters, if you're eating fruit bottom yogurt, swap in some plain yogurt and over time it will get easier.

Jennifer: Dave, what I learned to do with my kids, is I get frozen fruit now in a package of strawberries or raspberries. I put the puree into ice cube trays and then I dump the ice cubs into the yogurt for lunch. It melts in time and they've got a fruit yogurt. Again, it takes a little bit more work, but I totally believe our health is worth that.

Dave: That's cool, so inspiring. Jen, thanks again for taking the time to join us today, you're fantastic. For all the readers, in the *Resources* section, I will have links to Jen's website as well as her sugar swaps document.

Jennifer: Awesome. Dave, it's been so great talking with you. I hope the readers got some of their questions answered about this topic.

RESOURCES

Jennifer's Website: http://jenniferpowter.com

Jennifer's Sugar Swaps:
http://makeyourbodywork.com/jp-sugar-swaps

CHAPTER 8:

DOES YOUR WILLPOWER NEED A BOOST?

Wait a second.

In previous chapters, haven't we been talking about how willpower is NOT a solution for making healthier choices in life?

Yet, here we are. This entire chapter is dedicated to boosting your willpower. What gives?

I stand by my statement that willpower on its own is never enough to make long-lasting changes in any area of life. Eventually, your old habits will creep in, overcoming your desire to change.

However, willpower is an essential *component* of building long-lasting habits. Habits don't magically appear overnight. Your willpower will sustain you until those new, healthy habits usurp the old ones you want to overcome.

Sam knows this to be true from personal experience:

> *"I have zero willpower and dedication by dinnertime. I start out strong in the morning and go downhill from there. Some days I feel like I need to join Overeaters Anonymous. Is there something I need to change in my diet? Is it something else? I just need to stop going crazy in the evenings."*

Do you feel like Sam? Does your willpower have the strength to last a few hours (or maybe minutes) at most before you give in to whatever temptation you were hoping to avoid?

It's time to supercharge your willpower.

MEET BETSY PAKE

 Betsy is an entrepreneur, award winning business achiever, competitive weight lifter, and a success coach who hosts the popular podcast *The Art of Living Big*.

She's the author of the best selling book, *Become A Nutrition Ninja*, and she just released her latest book, *Start Small Live Big*. Betsy's mission is to help inspire others to thrive through change by starting small.

THE INTERVIEW

Dave: Hey, Betsy. Thanks so much for joining me.

Betsy: Yeah, thanks for having me.

Dave: I'm excited to have you as part of this book. We have a question today from Sam. As I learned a bit more about what you do and what your specialties are, I thought you'd be the perfect person to answer Sam's question. Before we dive into it, let's start talking about your book. It's called *Become a Nutrition Ninja*. What's that all about?

Betsy: I've been a nutrition coach for a long time. I'm a competitive athlete. I'm a masters level Olympic-style lifter. I found a lot of folks that were CrossFitters or Olympic lifters, had a lot of trouble gaining weight, or when they were trying to lean out. They wanted to look like all the hard work they put in, but they were having trouble.

What I wrote about is called flexible dieting, which is counting how much fat, protein, and carbohydrates you have daily. I map it out in this book, so people have an easy way to calculate their macros. This helps them get lean and show off all their hard work. I also use a few mindset techniques in my coaching program, but the flexible dieting is the basis of the book. I've successfully used it to drop several weight classes with my Olympic lifting program.

Dave: Very cool. Quick question for you about macronutrients: the protein, fat, and carbohydrates. Do the ratios change depending on the athlete you're working with, or are they generally the same across the board?

Betsy: It depends. I have trained some folks that have competed in an Ironman, and so their carbohydrate needs are much different than someone that's doing the Olympic lifting. It does depend on the athlete, but there are some generalities regarding how much protein you should have and that type of thing.

Dave: In the *Resources* section of this chapter, I'll put a link to *Become a Nutrition Ninja*, and you can take a look. It might be something you're interested in checking out.

Today's question is from Sam; I'll just recap. She talks about willpower and dedication to stay on what she calls a healthy eating plan. She says, "By the end of the day, I'm so worn out, I'll just eat anything." I love it. She jokes, saying she needs to join Overeaters Anonymous. When you read that, I'm sure you've dealt with clients who have had similar problems before?

WILLPOWER AND DEDICATION

Betsy: Yeah. That's a common problem people have. I know it's something I've struggled with as I've gone through my journey. About fourteen years ago—I'm not sure if you know this—but I gained about eighty pounds when I had my daughter, so I know what it is like to feel out of control and not like yourself. I think this is a common problem and, like I said, something I experienced.

I believe there are two basic ideas when I read this question. The first is successful people I have met and trained are people who, having an issue, figure out how to fix it, and the next day are up and back at it. That's number one. They continue and don't stop searching for an answer.

The other is something that crosses all different realms in your life. There's something called executive function. Throughout the day, every time you have to make a decision, whether about what you're going to eat or where to park in the mall, it depletes this executive function. It lowers your threshold to make and maintain great decisions by the end of the day.

The cool thing is that you can maintain this executive function and keep up your willpower by doing a couple of basic things. I talk to my coaching clients a lot about building a foundational schedule. For all of the little decisions you make every day that's the same decision, develop the foundational schedule so you no longer need to make those decisions. You make them once and lay that foundational schedule across every single day.

Dave: Maybe you can give an example. What would this look like in practice?

BUILDING A FUNDAMENTAL SCHEDULE

Betsy: An easy way to do this is building a foundational schedule around not only your food and choices throughout the day but also the things you do throughout the day. Talking about food, maybe there are certain snacks you have every single day at a particular time. You don't have to think about it. You prep those in advance, have them ready, and that's what you eat.

If you go into an office every day, pick an area of the parking lot where there aren't a lot of cars. You know you always park there. You always find a spot. It also gives you a chance to walk if it's farther away. Creating times and systems for things will help you preserve executive function, and give you more willpower by the end of the day.

Dave: I like the parking example because, although it seems unrelated to weight-loss or fitness, it's still one less decision you're making, something that's programmed.

Betsy: Yeah, and a decision can be something that's stressful. Maybe you're always looking for a parking spot, so you get frustrated and stressed. So much of eating and dieting is not about what you're eating, but what's in your head. If you're stressed and you're creating stressful, little environments throughout the day, it's going to affect what you're craving for food.

Dave: Yeah, that's interesting. I'm going to butcher this because it was a long time ago I read this. I read a research study that went something along the lines of consisting of two groups of people. One group was asked to do a very mentally demanding task, and the other group had a task that was not mentally demanding at all. As the groups left their respective rooms, they were offered either vegetables or

134

chocolate cake, and the group that had done the mentally demanding task overwhelmingly chose the chocolate cake.

Betsy: Yes, yes.

Dave: Have you heard of that before?

Betsy: Yeah, that's the same thing. Same kind of system.

Dave: Maybe you could give some more examples. I like the parking one, and as someone goes through the day they've got their parking spot and snacks programmed in. What other things would you have your clients incorporate to create that programming?

Betsy: I have some clients in sales, for example. They know there are certain daily tasks they have to do, but they're really in charge of their schedule. What I tell them, if you have to make phone calls to clients, set a time. Perhaps, every day between ten and twelve, that's what you do. Don't create a tiny stress bubble by trying to figure out or running out of time, and going, "Oh my gosh, I have to call these people. It's 4:30. What am I going to do?" Create that.

The other thing is to create a morning schedule. I tell all my clients to create a morning routine. Sometimes this is hard for them at first. I'll ask them to get up thirty minutes early. This gives them time when nobody else in the house is awake, where they can focus on planning themselves. Maybe that's meditation. I recommend that a lot. Maybe they read something important to them to fill them up.

Remember there's so much about our mindset that goes into our eating. How can you fortify yourself so when 10:00am comes, and you have to call these customers, you are fortified, strong, and ready to go? Now you're creating an environment that trickles down into your evening. Like Sam was saying, when she'd have those issues in the nighttime, now there's a schedule where you feel fortified. You feel good. You're mentally feeding yourself.

Now when it's time to make decisions at night, you're much stronger. Sometimes, our nighttime habits become a routine. It's a habit. If you always find yourself overeating at night, consider it a habit and break it like you would break any other habit.

EATING HABITS CAN BE CHANGED OR REPLACED

Dave: I love that. I interviewed a guest a couple of weeks ago, Renee Cefalu. She was very adamant about the statement we are not our habits, and we don't own those habits. Exactly like you just said, a habit is something that can be done away with. It's not us.

Betsy: Yeah. I always tell people, "Don't ignore the thing you don't want to do anymore." Actively find something to replace it. When a smoker wants to quit smoking, they suck on lollipops. It's the same kind of thing. Find something to replace it. I had a client who always needed a bowl of cereal right before they went to bed. We just replaced that with something else.

You start with little things. She would always have a cup, so then we decreased to a half-a-cup for a week. Then we went to a glass of milk, next to tea, and then it was gone. I feel like we beat ourselves up a lot. So, be kind to yourself and think through how you can actively make little changes to get the big change you want.

Dave: You just said a bunch of very powerful things. First of all, I liked the process you mentioned. It's basically breaking an addiction. You took the steps necessary to wean off the cereal addiction. It's funny you picked that. For years, I had an addiction to Raisin Bran. A bowl of Raisin Bran every night before bed. It was that same thing.

Betsy: Oh really? Yeah.

Dave: I wasn't hungry. I didn't need to eat it. It was just a very instilled habit.

Betsy: You'll have that, yeah.

Dave: I love the fact you gave a step-by-step process. And what you said at the end, I just want to reinforce it to the readers. Don't beat yourself up, and know it's something we all deal with like I just said about my Raisin Bran habit. Betsy, you said you gained eighty pounds during your pregnancy. Can you tell us about some of the habits that formed in your life?

HOW YOU ACQUIRE BAD EATING HABITS

Betsy: Yeah. I had two things I did every day. If you want to gain eighty pounds, do two things. There was a restaurant in the building where I worked, and I would go downstairs every day and get French fries. I never got French fries before. That wasn't my thing. It became a habit, and it was for comfort. After I had the baby, I realized it wasn't a baby on my thighs; it was French fries. I had to think about what was I doing actively.

Having this warm food at lunchtime was a comfort to me, so I had to replace it. I also joke about obsessing over chicken pot pies. I don't think I've had a chicken pot pie since pregnancy. It was a big habit for me because I knew I could pick it up on my way home. So, it was easy.

I had to think of what else was on my way home. What else would make this easy? How else can avoid them, like having to cook dinner myself? How else can I not have to cook dinner?

Creating, pre-planning, and planning meals out in advance. Asking for help. There are many things you can do to break your habits. You have to look back on the steps that lead to your habit and then figure out how to disrupt those steps. When you do that, you start to see changes.

Dave: Yeah, you mentioned some neat ideas. I liked what you said about the chicken pot pie and why did that. Maybe you didn't want to prepare dinner. I think that's very applicable to a lot of people who feel worn out by the end of the day. Picking up a pizza is easier than preparing dinner.

HAVE AN EMERGENCY PLAN

You said a solution is to have a plan, or prep ingredients on the weekend. I always say go-to meals, which don't require a lot of prep. There's a lot of things you can do.

Betsy: Yeah, and have an emergency plan. Say I didn't prep. I didn't get ready. I don't have anything in the house. I want to get a chicken pot pie. But I've already identified a Zoe's Kitchen next door where I'll get something healthy, so I'll go there instead.

THE PERFECTION CONTINUUM

Sometimes it's not about being perfect. It's a continuum. If perfect is on one end of the continuum and eighty pounds of pregnancy is on the other, what little choices can you make to move closer to perfection? You're never going to be perfect, but get closer to that end of the continuum.

Dave: I love that. I always tell my clients we're looking for progress, not perfection. Perfection doesn't even exist.

Betsy: I think we're so cruel to ourselves. We say things to ourselves we would never say to somebody else. We look in the mirror and say terrible things, thinking it will inspire us to do better.

Dave: Yes, that's interesting. Like you said, we'd never say it to someone else. We know it's a hurtful statement, but to say it to ourselves seems okay.

Betsy: Yeah. When my clients email me, they say, "Oh my gosh. This weekend I had a breakthrough. I looked at my thighs, and I didn't immediately think I hate them. I thought they were starting to look like I want. I'm getting stronger." When you make that shift, that's when the magic happens. That's when you're making lifelong changes.

Dave: I like that specific point because we're talking about getting leaner and this specific question is about eating healthier—but in reality, all those changes are for improved happiness and satisfaction with who we are as people. It's a great feeling when you look at your thighs and think they look stronger or you think you're okay. You're fine, and you're a good person. You like yourself.

Betsy: Yeah, it's a big transition, a big shift.

WHAT ABOUT THAT EVENING GLASS OF WINE?

Dave: This is a bit of a backtrack, but back to when we were talking about habits and routines around dinnertime. One of the questions I often get from clients is what to do with their evening glass of wine. I'm sure you've heard that from clients before too. Do you have a suggestion they can use as a replacement, or do they need a replacement? Do you tell your clients that?

Betsy: Yeah. It all depends on how it fits into your greater plan. With a lot of my clients, we work on macronutrients. If they have the macros for the wine, they can make a choice to have the wine. I always tell them I'd rather you have nourishing food instead of alcohol. There are times where you're going out, or you're meeting friends, and you've got to be able to live your life.

But I've talked to someone before who had a Pinot Grigio habit every night. So, we watered it down. We turned it into a spritzer, and then we turned it into more of a spritzer, using the same method of the continuum.

Dave: Did that client wean off it completely, or were they content with just keeping a watered-down version?

Betsy: The real story is she got pregnant, so she stopped cold turkey. It took care of that. The idea would have been to have one or two a week, yeah.

Dave: That's so practical. I'm sure there are a ton of readers who have an evening glass of wine. If it's something you want to change, then try. Try a little bit watered down, even if it's ten percent. It makes a difference.

Betsy: I'll get an email from clients, and it's someone who hasn't exercised in years. They've also been eating anything they want for the past five years, and they say, "I'm ready to change, and I want a diet plan. I want to work out five times a week. I want to track everything."

I'm like, "Whoa, whoa. I appreciate the excitement because I think that's important, but I want to go for a year. I want this to be a long-term thing." I always say pick a few things to work on. Maybe alcohol isn't one immediately. Maybe you keep it while you work on other things. I've had clients that were addicted to Mountain Dew.

Dave: Oh no.

Betsy: I've had someone addicted to Mountain Dew and cigarettes. Start with one or the other, but not both. We've got to be kind to ourselves and pick something. Maybe it takes a week, or maybe a month, but once it's no longer a habit, then add on and choose something else.

How to Sustain Willpower All Day Long

Dave: That's so relevant to Sam's question. She doesn't talk about her exercise, but she says by the end of the day, she doesn't have any willpower left. If someone were trying to take on multiple major shifts in life, of course, willpower wouldn't be there. If you had to bust your butt to get to the gym and that was already a battle and then you come home, expecting to cook yourself a healthy meal, good luck.

Betsy: Yeah, too much.

Dave: Betsy, I know we're just scratching the surface of your insights and wisdom, but where could people find out more about you and what you do?

Betsy: They can go to my website, betsypake.com, and I'm on social media everywhere at Betsy Pake. You can find me on Twitter and Instagram and all that good stuff.

Dave: Thanks for joining me. Like I said, I know we're just scratching the surface of what you can share with us, so hopefully readers will connect with you beyond this interview.

Betsy: Yeah, that sounds great. I'd love it.

RESOURCES

Betsy's Website: http://betsypake.com

Betsy's Book, *Becoming a Nutrition Ninja*: http://makeyourbodywork.com/betsy-ninja

CHAPTER 9:

WHERE DID YOUR ENERGY GO?

Have you ever noticed that it takes more energy to make healthy choices than it does unhealthy ones?

Preparing a healthy dinner requires energy. Ordering take-out doesn't.

Going to the gym requires a lot of energy while snuggling up on the couch with a glass of wine to watch Netflix is so relaxing.

Even going to bed can feel like it takes more energy than scrolling through your Facebook newsfeed.

Rita wants to know where all that energy is supposed to come from:

> *"Dave, here's a simple question for you. My energy, where did it go, and how can I get it to come back?"*

If your energy levels feel like they're at an all-time low, don't sit idly by. There are 5 ways you can naturally boost your energy so that healthy decisions are much more doable every day.

Meet Karen Wojciechowski

Karen Wojciechowski is a health coach who studied at the Institute for Integrative Nutrition. She has traveled much of the world and currently resides in the city of Perth, Australia.

Her online programs, focused on whole-food eating, have allowed her to work with people across the globe, making a worldwide impact, especially in the area of restoring natural energy.

The Interview

Dave: Hey, Karen. Thanks so much for joining me for this interview today.

Karen: Thanks so much for having me.

Dave: Yeah, I'm excited to have you. I get questions all the time about energy levels, so let's talk about Rita's question. She says, "My energy's died. Where did it go?" That's something I hear all the time, and the more I've read about you online, the more I realized you love helping people find their energy.

Karen: Yeah, I love helping people boost their energy levels because when you feel tired or fatigued, you don't have the energy to make great healthy habits to help you with all the other aspects of your life. You don't feel like exercising, and if you're tired, you'll crave more sugary foods. Thus, it's harder to eat healthily.

All the things I help people with to boost their energy can flow into other aspects of their life. They might be focusing on increasing their energy, but they've lost a couple of pounds that have been sticking around, or their digestion feels better. I love helping people boost their energy and their health because there is an effect on all the other aspects of their life,

Dave: How did you come across that? When you say that, it makes sense. When we have good energy we'll make better healthy life choices, but how did you figure that out?

Karen: Yeah, I started to realize whenever you ask people, "How's it going?" or you talk to them, it seems like everybody was either busy or tired. It was the standard answer. I think there's this perception that if you're not busy, tired, and stressed out, you're not trying hard enough. I wanted to shake that up and help people enjoy life. To be happier through helping them focus on things to boost their energy levels.

Dave: I love that you just said that. One thing I've noticed as I get older in life is we look at busyness as a badge of honor. If I'm busy, therefore I'm important, or I've got something neat going on in my life. I've often thought about when people say, "How are you doing?" of replying with, "Great. I didn't do that much this week," and just see their reaction.

Karen: Yeah, I completely agree. It is almost like a badge of honor, and it so doesn't have to be. Slowing down and enjoying what you are doing doesn't have to be a bad thing. That can be a good thing, and it's a healthy thing, you know?

Dave: Yeah. Obviously, we're going to get into the practical side of this, but first, let's get back to Rita. She says, "My energy level, where did it go, and how can I get it to come back?" When you hear someone say that—which you obviously do all the time—what's the first thing you dive into? Where do you look?

LISTEN TO THE MESSAGE COMING FROM YOUR BODY

Karen: The first thing I'd say to somebody who's coming in saying, "Yeah, my energy levels are really low," is to think of feeling tired or feeling fatigued in a different way.

I like to think about it as a message from your body. I want people to think about all these symptoms, including tiredness, like the way your body is communicating with you. It wants you to do something different.

It might want you to eat or drink differently, move more, or even breathe and think in a different way. I want people thinking about these like messages your body is giving you. So don't attach guilt or willpower.

You're just listening like your body is trying to communicate with you, and that's a good thing. It's given me a signal I need to change something up before the symptoms get worse or something happens down the line. The first thing I get people to do is to think about it as a good thing your body is telling you and then let's try to figure out what you need to do.

Dave: That's a neat perspective because when you think about the ways your body can communicate with you, there aren't many. It can send out pain, you can have digestive issues, fatigue, but beyond that, there isn't much. So, like you said, it's your body crying out, "Hey, pay attention."

Karen: Exactly.

Dave: That's interesting. When you start to work with a client to discover what the root is, or what your body is trying to say, how do you begin the process?

Karen: When somebody comes to me, and they are struggling with something like this, then we start to look at factors. There's a bunch of things that contribute to fatigue, but some of the areas we start with are food. What are you eating? We also look at movement and exercise. They are big energy boosters.

We look at what you are drinking: water, coffee, and the like. Next are sleep and stress. Think of your sleep and where you are regarding stress. Those five things often have the largest impact on your energy levels.

WATCH OUT FOR ENERGY DEPLETING FOODS

Dave: Yeah, I would agree, but when you think about those five, they're very broad. That's pretty comprehensive, so maybe we could start with food, and you can give some ideas to the readers. What can they start to look for? Are specific foods energy detractors? Are there ones people should think about eating more of?

Karen: It is broad, but my philosophy regarding food is to eat real food whenever possible. We look for where people can add in more real foods and crowd out what, as you said, contributes to energy depletion.

Sugar can deplete your energy. It's a huge one. Sugar and caffeine drain energy enormously. I know people hate it when I say caffeine because we're all addicted to morning coffee or—for some people—three or four coffees throughout the day.

Sugar can also be tough to give up for people. But having too much of those two can have a massive impact on your energy levels. From both, you get spikes of energy—but it also crashes you, which causes cravings. Then, the cycle starts again where you have coffee in the morning or throughout the day, sugar in the afternoon, and then you need your glass of wine in the evening to wind down. It isn't great for having all day energy.

Dave: You are making enemies all over the place. Coffee, sugar, and wine all in one sentence.

Karen: I do tend to make some enemies with comments like that.

Dave: Maybe you could give the readers some hope. Say someone was addicted to caffeine—it was their booster every morning—but wanted to wean off it or stop altogether. Typically, how long does it take your clients before their body compensates and has a natural boost of energy as opposed to relying on a stimulant?

FOOD: ADD IN TO CROWD OUT

Karen: Everybody's different, and it depends on how much coffee you're drinking, but I tend to wean people off slowly. To be honest, I'm not saying everybody needs to quit coffee or those other things.

I want people to focus on crowding out what isn't ideal for them by adding in what is helpful to their bodies and good for energy levels.

When taking caffeine out, we reduce it slowly and get to where people are only having one or two cups a day. For some people, removing caffeine altogether makes them feel a lot better, but everybody is different. It depends on how the person is dealing with some of those other things we talked about.

If someone is in a stressful job, and it's having an impact on their energy levels, then caffeine may not help their energy levels. It's likely something they need to cut out. But somebody who doesn't have as many issues or stress, having one to two cups of coffee a day could be healthy for them.

Dave: I like that message of a unique approach. What you just said, it resonates so strongly with all of the other guests I interview. There is no cookie-cutter approach, no matter what it is you're trying to accomplish.

Karen: Totally, and I wish there were. It would make everything a lot easier.

Dave: Then there would be no book, save for one chapter: Do this.

Karen: Totally, and that's not the way it works at all.

Dave: I wanted to follow up with something you said because you gave some good wisdom about the idea of crowding out what we want to wean off of. What are some things you would recommend people use to crowd out coffee, sugar, wine, or whatever it is?

Karen: I focus on crowding out so we can focus on what we are adding in rather than thinking about restricting or avoiding. I believe once you start to add in more healthy things, you naturally want less sugar or caffeine. It's then easier to make a long-term sustainable change. I love helping people make habits to set them up for the long-term.

If we're looking at coffee, drinking more water can help with your energy levels. It's fascinating how many people either forget or just don't drink water and going around dehydrated. If you're drinking more water and feeling better, then you don't need much caffeine.

Also, eat healthy greens, perhaps a green smoothie in the morning so you're adding in more vegetables. That makes you feel more energized. You'll begin to rely less on the coffee and the sugar. Healthy fats are also necessary. Lots of people shy away from healthy fats.

Add in lots of greens, veggies, some healthy fat, healthy protein, drink lots of water, throw in a green smoothie, and there are lots of options.

Drink teas, or maybe some hot water and lemon, or even kombucha. It's not a warm drink, but it's something good for you. Or make homemade hot chocolates with some raw cacao. Or turmeric tea with cinnamon, nutmeg, and honey with a bit of almond milk. I give people all these options to include rather than focusing on taking out.

Dave: Great ideas. I like the idea of turmeric tea. Turmeric has so many health benefits, especially reducing inflammation. I love that one.

Karen: Yeah, it's really good. You should try it. There are a couple of cafes around here that have started to have it on their menu, which is awesome. I was so excited the first time I walked into a café and saw a turmeric tea made just like I described. Even in a café, you can go out and have this amazing, healthy option instead of coffee.

My Own Fat-Deficiency Experience

Dave: I love that. One thing that I wanted to mention. It hit close to home when you were speaking about eating healthy fats. About twenty or twenty-one, I went through a year or two where I had terrible sleep problems and was chronically fatigued all the time.

At the pinnacle, I realized I had an issue when on a conference call at work I fell asleep. I woke up because I was drooling all over the receiver of the phone. I was like, "This isn't normal. Something's wrong." Long story short, I saw a ton of different doctors and was on several prescription medications. But nothing was working, and eventually it was through diet that I "healed myself."

I was fat deficient. The more I studied it and learned about fat soluble vitamins, I realized I was so restrictive to my body. All I did was start adding in nuts, seeds, avocado, cooking with a lot more oil, and literally in a month I was healed. It's a testament to how your diet dictates how your body functions.

Karen: Wow. Isn't that amazing? It's such an amazing story of how these things can have such a significant impact.

THE CONSEQUENCES OF LIVING WITH LOW ENERGY

Dave: Yeah, and before this interview, you and I were talking about some of the symptomatology people might experience when low energy creeps in. You mentioned weight gain is one of them. When people are low energy, all these lifestyle choices translate into gaining weight. And then, people see that as the problem and want to tackle the weight, when in reality, it's just a symptom.

Karen: Totally. They're connected. If you feel tired all the time, you're don't want to go to the gym, or go for a walk, or do anything involving exercise.

Often when you feel tired, you're going to crave things like sugar to give you quick energy. So, it's much harder to stick to a regular, healthy eating lifestyle when you're tired all the time.

It's also harder to meal plan, prep food, or even cook. You will likely grab takeout or go with the easy option because you're so tired. People don't realize they can have more energy.

I've had somebody say to me before, "I work full time, so isn't it normal I come home from work at five and be too tired to do anything?" I'm like, "Well, no. We can get you to the stage where that doesn't happen." They say, "Oh, no. I work full time, so isn't that normal I'm just going to be exhausted at 5?" I tell them, "No. You're too young. That's too early to feel so tired." People are amazed at how much better they can feel. But before then, they might focus on other things like weight-loss or the symptoms of having low energy levels.

Dave: It's interesting when you talk about someone who says, "Well, isn't this normal?" When something changes over a very extended period of time, we often don't realize we're in poor health. The idea of something being better than what we're experiencing is hard to believe because it might have been ten years since we experienced something like that.

Again, I can just relate. I remember myself all of the sudden thinking I was weird, and I shouldn't be falling asleep on the phone. But other than that I didn't even realize it.

We talked about food and some of the replacements you can use to crowd out some of the unhealthy energy boosters. What about exercise? What do you recommend to your clients?

USE MOVEMENT TO BOOST YOUR ENERGY

Karen: Just get moving because every client is different. It totally depends on where they are currently. How much are they exercising? Do we just need to get them off the couch and go for a thirty-minute walk every day? Is it going to make them feel better?

It also depends if stress is significant for them. I think stress can be detrimental when it comes to energy levels. Those people will need restorative practice.

Maybe doing yoga a few times a week will have more benefits than an hour on the treadmill or lifting weights.

Everybody is different, but at the same time, doing any exercise is huge for energy boosting. Anything you do to build muscle can help with energy boosting as well. Doing some resistance exercises, even if it's only body weight exercises, squats, or simple exercises at home can help as well.

Dave: Thank you for mentioning the fact something like yoga or more gentle forms of exercise is okay. I know it's a pet peeve of mine. I think we've been done a disservice to some people with all of the high-intensity workout programs. People expect exercise to look like that, but your message says it doesn't have to.

Karen: No, not at all. As we were saying with food, everybody is different; exercise is the same. Some of those high-intensity workouts might not be ideal for somebody who is struggling with symptoms of stress. They might benefit more from something like yoga or some of other restorative practices. I'm a big fan of yoga. Yoga is amazing, and it can be a great workout, too.

Dave: I totally agree. I'm not taking anything away from yoga. It's different, and unless you're doing hot yoga, it's not like you're dripping in sweat. In most cases at least.

Karen: No, totally. I agree. I just like to encourage people to do more exercise and start moving, get up throughout their day, sit less, things like that.

KEY ENERGY BOOSTER: DRINK MORE WATER!

Dave: Nutrition, movement, and what was number three on your list?

Karen: Drink more water. Simple, but decreases energy levels for those people that aren't drinking enough.

Dave: Do you have a baseline you recommend?

Karen: As a minimum, you want to drink half your body weight in ounces of water. But it depends on how active you are and your climate. I get people to check their water for me, then we look and help them start drinking enough.

Dave: I remember I heard a personal trainer giving a talk about hydration, and he said, "Drink 'til your pee don't stink." That's stuck with me, and this is personal, but when I go to the washroom, I always look at it and think, "How yellow was it? Did it have that urine smell in it?" I think that's a helpful rule of thumb.

Karen: I like that. I do the same. Yeah, that's entirely true. I do check it out like, "Oh, maybe I should be drinking more water." That's a great rule of thumb for all you readers.

Dave: Okay, good. We both just grossed everyone out. Thank you. Drinking water was number three. Number four?

ARE YOU GETTING ENOUGH SLEEP?

Karen: Sleep. Get some sleep. Sleep can be a huge topic on its own. People need to see sleep as a health activity, like exercise. It's important, so prioritize it. Blacking out the room is crucial.

Improve the quantity of your sleep wherever you can, but also improve the quality. Make sure you're in a dark room and turn off all screens. It's hard for people. If you can, an hour or two before you go to bed, have an evening routine to ease you to sleep.

Sleep is big when it comes to fatigue, and I think people have a lot of trouble with sleep today.

Dave: You know what I liked? The mindset shift you gave. Think of sleep as a health activity just like you would exercise.

Karen: Yeah, because it is. Sometimes it might be more beneficial to get a couple of extra hours of sleep than wake up and hit the gym. I'm all for incorporating exercise wherever we can, but sleep is important.

Dave: I love that. I am taking that away for myself. I would never miss a workout, but I would easily sacrifice two hours of sleep if I were extremely busy.

Karen: If you're sacrificing two hours of sleep because you're busy one day but usually sleep well, you probably won't notice a difference. If you know of a night where you will sleep less, then try to bank it up.

Sleep a little extra leading up to the night when you will sleep less. It might sound over-organized, but planning your sleep for the week like you plan your workouts has many restorative benefits. It can be vital, and people will notice a real difference when they're not sleeping well. I'm a big fan of sleep.

Dave: I think it'd be so awesome if you could lie down and flip this sleep button. "Okay, tonight I'm going to get eight hours. Tomorrow I'm only getting six, so I'll get ten the next night." That'd be great.

Karen: Yeah, it's harder in practice, but people can at least think about it and prioritize it.

HOW TO REDUCE YOUR STRESS

Dave: Karen, you said number five was working on reducing stress, correct?

Karen: Yeah, stress is ruinous to your energy levels. Earlier, we were talking about how everybody is busy and stressed out these days.

When you're stressed, you're taking a lot of short, sharp, shallow breaths, so getting people to do deep breathing when they're stressed or think about how they're breathing can be helpful. Meditation practice and yoga help with this. If we can

153

bring just a few of these little things in, they will decrease stress levels and boost energy. Stress can feed into how you're sleeping, eating, and moving, so it's paramount to work with someone through these things.

Dave: Now, Karen, you've been generous already, but you've got a gift for all of the readers. Maybe you could quickly tell us about that, and where can they go to claim theirs?

Karen: Yeah, I've got a *3-Day Energy Boosting Detox*. I've got some recipes in there for you. I've also got some non-food challenges to get your energy levels going in three days. You can just go ahead and go to realenergyfood.com/energy.

Dave: Great, and I'll put that in the *Resources* section at the end of this chapter. Karen, I appreciate it. Thanks so much for sharing your wisdom.

Karen: Awesome.

RESOURCES

Karen's Website: http://realenergyfood.com

Karen's Free 3-Day Detox:
http://makeyourbodywork.com/kw-energy
Karen's Recommended Turmeric Tea Recipe: http://makeyourbodywork.com/kw-tumeric-tea

CHAPTER 10:

CAN YOU RE-START YOUR METABOLISM?

So far we've talked a lot about different strategies for losing weight. We've touched on food choices, exercise, mindset, stress-reduction, and many others.

But, what if these tactics used to work for you, but suddenly don't anymore? Is it possible that your body has completely changed, and there is no going back?

That's what Sandra feared:

> *"How does getting older impact weight loss and building muscle? I've been working out very hard for awhile now, eating right, cutting out sugar as much as possible, increasing fiber and good fats, incorporating both weights and body weight exercises, doing some cardio, adding all these things to my life, yet still in the last few years losing weight has been almost impossible. I've even had my thyroid checked to see if that was the problem, but nothing seems to connect.*
>
> *So my thoughts are that age must be a factor. I'm now 42 years old. What can I do to counteract this and get my metabolism to kick in again?"*

MEET DEBRA ATKINSON

Debra Atkinson is a life and fitness coach who has been nicknamed "America's Boomer Babe Fitness Expert" because of her expertise in helping women lose weight and get in great shape during their 40s, 50s, and beyond.

She holds her B.S. and M.S. in Exercise Science and Exercise & Sports Psychology, has been a motivational speaker for over 30 years, and currently hosts "Flipping 50" TV.

THE INTERVIEW

Dave: Hey Debra. Thanks so much for joining me today.

Debra: Thanks so much for having me.

Dave: Before we get started, I want you to tell the readers about your show because you've got a pretty neat show on the go.

Debra: Well, two fold. There is the FlippingFifty show that's a podcast, but the really exciting thing for me, and I think for readers, will be the FlippingFifty TV show. Really what I do is take questions from my subscribers, viewers, fans, and we literally answer one.

While I'm much more digital than I ever used to be and I don't get a lot of face-to-face time, it's so much fun because I really am thinking about that person in my head the entire show and answering their question knowing there's somebody else who has that question out there.

We literally dive in and say here's my exercise solution for you, but here's a something else you need to think about because often it's about sleep or another lifestyle habit that pulls into how successful that exercise will be for them.

Dave: That's the same format that I use for my podcast. I don't know if you've experienced this as well, but sometimes I'll get questions that seem really unique and I'll think, "Oh that's interesting, I'll find an expert and we'll answer that."

Meanwhile, in my head I'm thinking, "Okay, this is so unique there's no way anyone else cares about this question." It's usually those ones that I get a response from other people saying, "I've been waiting to hear an answer to that!" or, "I've been searching for an answer."

Have you found that as well?

Debra: So true. Yeah. One of the things that really stands out when you say that is the forgotten group of people. Every article, every blog, every advertisement, and program target women, in particular who are my crowd, who want to lose weight. There is also this group of women who now find it hard to hold onto weight, to create shape. When I got a question like that, I think, "Gosh, do I have enough people who will care?" and so many people, like you said, were like, "Thank you because nobody pays attention to us!"

Dave: You said, "your crew." Who is your crew?

Debra: Generally I work with females who are approaching 50, turn the corner on 50, and hormones start calling the shots. What they've done before that worked isn't working anymore, or if they felt like they didn't have to pay attention earlier in their life, they suddenly do.

It's helping them reframe their exercise so it addresses hormone balance and it is much less focused on calories in and out. As you know, we're not built as a math formula so much as we're a chemistry lab. There is no easy equation to follow.

Dave: I was wondering, does this whole focus on "flipping fifty" and dealing with hormones and stuff, does this have anything to do with your personal story, or why did you start to work with this group?

WHY 50? DEBRA'S PERSONAL STORY

Debra: Oh, you're getting personal now. Okay. So smooth. All right. It does and it doesn't. I always have felt this kindred spirit with older adults because I was raised by older parents. I was the youngest of four children so my mom had me when it wasn't popular and sexy to have a baby at 36, way back when, and then she remarried somebody 10 years older than she was.

If you can understand this, I grew up with the "Rat Pack." That's who he played golf with and that's who I hung out with. I think I was older because of that. Even as a 20-year-old, I was older. I loved that crowd because they're so appreciative. It's more than vanity, it's more than weight-loss, and they know it. Then yes, at 49 years old, I had a midlife crisis. I'm 52 now, so I have survived my crisis!

It was very uncomfortable though. If felt like I was squeezing through a tight tube, and then I finally got out on the other end and it's like, "If I didn't do that I wouldn't have grown like I grew," which means there was a lot of pain along the way.

I made all these life changes at a time when physically, at 49, things are drastically changing. Hormones are changing under the hood so going through additional stressors during that time, it's not something I would recommend, but it's what happened to me.

What I realized along the way was that my old patterns of loving exercise and needing more than some others do, really was no longer possible. There were days when I fit in 20 minutes, that was it, so I had to really make it count. I couldn't exercise for an hour or more every day. It just didn't work for me any longer.

What I found however, is my fitness level, my energy level, body composition, my weight, stayed the same as when I had been training for marathons and Iron Man distance triathlons. I was able to exercise less, but still remain fit and lean.

WHAT'S HAPPENING TO MY BODY?

Dave: Interesting. I am a little bit different age category in that I'm in my later thirties now, but I've noticed very similar things. I just say this to the readers, Debra, you focus specifically on women around that 50-year-old mark, but this applies to all of us as we age. Our metabolism starts to change. The thing that I've really noticed in the five years is my body's ability to recover. I used to be able to push myself and work out, do exercise twice a day and all this crazy stuff and I just can't do it anymore.

Debra: Yeah. Totally agree. In the book I wrote, *You Still Got It, Girl! The After 50 Fitness Formula for Women*, and not that it doesn't, like you said, apply to all of us, that's one of the chapters. It's probably the least sexy chapter to read. People dive right into the exercise or dive right into the nutrition, but making sure that you recover before you do the next workout is so foreign to us. We live in this world of push, push, push, do more.

Dave: Particularly as our bodies age, and again I really notice this myself is, my body can store fat more easily than it could five years ago. The natural tendency is to say, "Okay, I'm going to work harder to prevent that from happening," but it's a real struggle because simultaneously as we age we need to work out smarter, not harder, and then also do other things that will compensate for that natural propensity to store fat. It's a challenging equation.

Debra: Yeah. Right. That was the bonus you didn't ask for, right, the increased ability to store fat.

Dave: Yeah, yeah. Exactly. I don't know if I'll call that a bonus.

Debra: I know. It's so true. For women, I think we come back to the fact that rest and recovery tie right into stress. Not that you men are not, but us women can't shut our monkey brains off. Women have a harder time doing that. We could be in the boardroom doing major deals and in charge, but we're also thinking about "Did somebody leave that bowl of chilli in the sink? Is it getting crusty?"

We can't help it. We're just like, uh 30 things at once going on in our heads and that increases our cortisol level because we can't focus on one purpose unless we practice it. Learning how to decrease our stress level, really be present, is a huge part of it as well as the physical recovery that we need.

Dave: We've already started to touch on some of the areas that might address Sandra's specific question, but basically she says, "I'm 42 and I'm noticing all these changes. Losing weight's harder, and building muscle is harder."

She's been trying and she lists all the things that she's doing. She's doing a lot of those "right things" but still nothing, she says, "Nothing seems to connect." It must be such a common question or common statement for the demographic that you work with. What do you do? What's your advice?

WHEN THE DOTS DON'T SEEM TO CONNECT

Debra: A couple things here that I want to call attention to. She says, " I've had my thyroid checked to see if that was the problem, but nothing seems to connect." Sometimes thyroid testing doesn't show up with accurate results, so what I would encourage anybody to do is to trust their signs and symptoms. Those won't lie.

Sometimes it takes up to 90 percent damage to your thyroid in order for it to show up on a test, so instead, I would ask about your sleep level. How is your sleep *quality* on a scale from one to 10 before you go into the number of hours. Sometimes I'll hear people are sleeping eight hours, but they're waking up 15 times so we know it's not quality. We want to consider quality and quantity.

Do you have trouble getting to sleep? Staying asleep? Do you wake too early? Are you in bed all night and think you got a good night sleep, but you wake up still hungover, not feeling like you're rested?

Those signs and symptoms kind of point to thyroid, but really, the first stop in your journey is your adrenal glands. They may be signalling that you're starting to burn out.

I agree with all the steps she's already taken - increasing fiber, cutting out sugar as much as possible, incorporating good fats, bodyweight exercise, doing some cardio, and all those good things.

However, sometimes I think stepping back, if you feel like you're doing everything right, take an easy slow week where you get outside and you get some life balance and perspective back. Let go of driving, driving, driving and that focus on "I can't get what I want," and just letting it go for a little bit, to trust and tune in to when you're sleepy, when you're tired, when you're hungry, when you're thirsty. Take some notes on all of those things to see where you are in a week and then gradually reintroduce exercise along with your other good habits. You might need to shake things up a little bit and this is one way to approach that.

Dave: I think that's really cool because asking someone to start tracking sleep, tracking how their body feels, tracking digestion versus eating habits, all that stuff, it sounds like extra work. It's neat what you just suggested there is maybe taking a week off and being okay with maybe not spending as much time exercising as you normally would and replace that time with some of this mindful activity or tuning in with yourself. Maybe those insights will be there.

Debra: Agree. Yep. What I do in one of my programs is say, "Alright, this first week I'm really going to ask you to make some strong changes in nutrition. This is going to be some work. I want you to Google about your foods and how much fiber is in them. I can tell you how much fiber's in certain foods, but it's really beneficial for you to go through that painstaking task, look it up every time."

We eat a lot of repeats. Yes, you're right, doing that kind of homework, just let that replace some of your exercise time and pay a lot of attention to your tracking results and let the exercise go for that week. Not that you're not going to be active, but you'll be spending less focused time exercising for that week.

This brings up a really good topic that I think you and I should probably focus on here. Sandra says she's working very hard now trying to do some things. My question is always what's the rest of your life look like when you're not exercising?

Dave: What are you getting at there? In terms of what?

DO YOU HAVE ANY N.E.A.T. IN YOUR LIFE?

Debra: Yeah. I'm getting at N.E.A.T., the Non-Exercise Activity Time. I'm a strong proponent of the idea that results are, in as far as obesity goes, not just related to your formal exercise time. It's not just half an hour or an hour of formal exercise, get your heart rate up and go hard, but it's really the other 23 and a half or 23 hours of the day when are you getting up frequently from your desk if you do have a sedentary job, you are standing a portion of that time, you are taking advantage of your lunch hour to walk somewhere. Those types of N.E.A.T. activities make a difference.

Maybe doing a little activity, walking down the hall, walking at lunch, taking advantage of every opportunity to be an active person, not just be an exerciser. A lot of the research data tells us that the correlation between those people who are more active in their daily life and optimal body weight is higher than those people who simply formally exercise but sit still the rest of the day.

Dave: It's very easy to check that exercise box and then think, "I went for a run today, therefore I can eat whatever I want and do whatever I want the rest of the day."

It doesn't work that way. Not at all, not at all.

You probably hear people say this and as do I, it is exactly that. "I kicked butt in my workout today and therefore I'm going to go and eat _____." Unfortunately the equation doesn't play out that way.

Debra: That's right. It really doesn't. I think it's okay to enjoy a treat, I find nothing wrong with that. I think if you can get into lifestyle habits where you're flipping, I call it flipping of course, that's my language, or swapping, making swaps for...you know let's give up the soda and if you're still needing some kind of treat, sparkling water with a little Stevia and lemon so you've got something that feels a little bubbly, a little bit sweet, but it's not quite so bad, so we're moving you down the continuum, getting away from the desire for some of those things.

There's a quote that a recent client gave me. She was like, "I like feeling good." I thought that's pretty brilliant. That's really all we need to know. That was just her way of saying, "I'm not going back, I like feeling good."

TWEAKING YOUR DIET BASED ON PROTEIN SYNTHESIS

Dave: I'd like to really drill down and give Sandra some specifics so that she can feel good too. Again, I love your suggestion of taking that week to reflect. What are some specific questions that Sandra, or anyone else in this situation, should be asking? Or, what are some specific things that she and anyone else should be tracking?

Debra: Great question. One of the things she mentions is about eating right. That one sometimes to me is a little grey. It means something different to everybody, so I would deep dive into what that mean for her.

Dave, I think it's perfectly fine if you and I have differing views on this, but one of the things I know about women I work with is they're all a little bit confused about how much protein they need and how to get in enough. Often we think, or we assume, that we get plenty of protein. We can read articles that say these are high-protein foods, but it's all relative.

The research that's used most often came from way back in 2008, and the RDAs (recommended daily allowance) haven't changed, and it'll be a long time before they do unfortunately.

Protein is number one. I would ask how many grams of protein do you have at your breakfast, at your lunch, and at your dinner. Not a total at the end of the day, but how much at each meal. There is an optimal for muscle protein synthesis.

You need to target an amount of protein that will help you prevent losses as you age, and will help you make gains in lean muscle, which will boost your metabolism.

We need about 28 grams of protein, maybe a little bit less, at each meal. If you're really active you don't need as much because you're body is better at synthesizing the protein.

An athletic body is easier or does better at synthesizing protein than does a sedentary body. This is not very intuitive. Most people think, "Well, I'm not very active so I don't need very much protein," but it's the reverse. I would look at that.

Here's what I use, is between 20 and 30 grams is a range at breakfast and at lunch and at dinner. Are you getting that? That may be something that we need to look at.

Dave: You said something really interesting, you said, "…at each meal" and then you specifically said, "…not your daily total." The typical standard we hear all the time is "Eat this many grams of protein per day."

Debra: Right.

Dave: Why do you say "per meal" instead?

Debra: It's about that muscle protein synthesis. At one time, your body can only handle so much. It's a little like how we've always talked about vitamins. You take a vitamin in the morning and if you use the restroom and you check, it's probably a lot more yellow, right?

Dave: Yeah.

Debra: You know that you're flushing some of those vitamins down the toilet because your body can't process so much at one time. By taking in between 20 and 30 grams you're hitting that optimal amount your body can use to build your muscles, meaning it's enough, but also that it's not too much.

The typical American diet, and I realize I'm talking to a Canadian so I can't speak for you, you all may be doing it better than we do, but the typical American diet includes very little protein at breakfast. All of our breakfast foods are very high in carbs traditionally.

A little bit more protein at lunch, and then most people really indulge in protein at night. The total could look about the same as getting a third of each at every meal, but your body can't use it as well. We need that sweet spot of protein at every meal to go to the use of your muscles.

VARIETY IS THE SPICE OF LIFE!

Dave: You described that perfectly. Just a little side note here: I quite often get people when they're asking me about what type of protein supplement to use, and personally I really like vegan sources. There's fermented vegan protein supplement that I love, I think it's great for most people's digestion.

When I recommend that to clients, quite often I'll have them coming from a place where they're using whey and they will look at the labels and say, "My whey has 28 grams per scoop of protein and this vegan one only has 18, so it's not as good."

But, if you're thinking about getting that 20 to 30 grams per meal, jeez throw in an 18 gram scoop of protein supplement, you're going to get in that range no problem.

Debra: Right. Absolutely. I agree with you. I'm a meat eater. There's something to be said about whey at other times of day when it might not be ideal because it is so rapidly absorbed it can spike blood sugar in somebody who has that tendency anyway. There's a proper timing to it.

For a lot of the women I work with, if they don't handle dairy well, they have to be reminded whey protein is dairy so you want to look at that. I love rotating. Definitely not having the same thing in any way every single day. You want a variety of nutrients.

Having some vegan or plant-based protein one day, having a ... I also use a beef protein, so it's not quite your beef collagen, but it's a beef protein that's animal source but not dairy, nor do I use soy. Rotating your protein with whey if your stomach can tolerate it. You get a broad variety of nutrients, which is also something that's really smart to do. You need so many different micronutrients, not the same ones every day.

Dave: Agreed. Rotating protein sources is a great step, as is rotating our food choices in general.

Now, before the show Debra, you and I were talking a little bit about sleep and I was wondering if maybe you could address that. How is Sandra, or someone else who's listening who can resonate with Sandra's message, supposed to track sleep for that week that you suggested they take for self-reflection? How can they track sleep? What should they be looking for?

How Does Your Sleep Stack Up?

Debra: Yeah. Great question. What I have people do is called a "Sleep Needs Test." This actually came from Dr. Michael Breus, "The Sleep Doctor." It's basically you have to give yourself a little time. It works so much better if you're taking a few days off from work, which people might be doing over, say, a long weekend or if they can take a holiday or maybe work for themselves and the boss will give them a break in the morning.

At night, pay attention to when your eyelids really start to droop. Don't try to stay up until the next commercial or the news is over or think it's just too early to go to bed. You're body's telling you it's time, go and write that down, what time was it.

Then, if you can, control everything possible in your environment, the noise, the darkness. If you have a snoring partner you may need to separate for a night or two to get a good night sleep. You may have to kick the dog out. I know that feeling. Up and down and up and oh my gosh. I sleep better away at a hotel and most people are the opposite.

Then you want to say, "Okay, I'm going to let myself wake up naturally" and then record that time. What you're looking for is the time you get sleepy, the time you go to bed, the time you woke up, and then look at what's the time in between. Write a little bit about quality of your night-time sleep. Did you wake many times or at all? What was it like, and how do you feel in the morning?

If you can get three to five days of this testing, you will begin to see some patterns. Look at your averages. What was your bedtime? Your wake time? What's the total average amount of sleep that you really needed and now look at what's true. How much are you really giving yourself and is there a gap? If you're short-changing yourself an hour night's sleep, by the end of the week you've lost an entire night's sleep! You're really deprived and you can't function as well when you're sleep deprived. Your body can't lose weight as easily either.

Dave: I love that you brought this up. Dr. Breus is actually one of the experts I am interviewing in this series, so readers can learn more about this process in chapter 13 of this book.

Debra, I love the fact that you emphasized finding that time, that ideal time, to go to bed and time to wake up and not just thinking about it as I need to get X number of hours to sleep. Can you tell the readers Debra about your bedtime?

Debra: Yeah, no. He's really pulling back the curtain here everybody. Be careful what you say to this guy because it'll come back to bite you. Yeah. My eyes go at about 8pm. It's winter as we're doing this interview and I'm "solar powered," so I sleep with the sun going down.

In the summer I'll go to bed around 9pm, but sun is just barely going down then, but that's my best. I wake up naturally about four. I have a four-legged friend who, if I'm not awake by five, will let me know meaning it's time, there's something out there we need to be doing today.

I really have to listen. Like you, I can get caught up in a movie and I can fight it, but I've got to remind myself that I'm going to regret this tomorrow, not because I won't be able to function, but because I really won't feel my best. There is a huge difference. Do you mind if I share a story here, Dave?

Dave: Yeah. Please do.

A MOTIVATIONAL SUCCESS STORY

Debra: If you need a little motivation here it is. I've been working with a particular client and I'll share her name, she won't mind, Jennifer, for two and a half years now. I was running a state-wide challenge and she was selected to be one of the people in the group. She struggled a lot. She was exercising a lot, three to four hours a day, she was eating sometimes just 800 to 1,000 calories. She was well into the upper 200lb level and was really struggling with injury, injury after injury, go figure.

We really had to work on her mindset. After making some shifts, she was eating over twice as much, exercising less than half as much, and taking, and you should gasp right here, two days off a week! I say that you should gasp because she was exercising seven days before. This was all very scary for her because it wasn't intuitive. She was from the discipline of, "If I work harder I will get better results."

We shifted all of that and she saw some progress, she certainly felt better, but the weight was still not coming off. The last straw her sleep. She was waking a lot throughout the night, and we knew this from a Fitbit.

I said, "You know what? The best of the best is that you sleep without any sleep supplement, but it's just not happening right now so let's go explore that."

She did. She started on a small dose of something to support her sleep, and now she's a new woman. In the last year she's lost close to 60 pounds that has come off much more easily since she's been getting a full night's sleep.

Dave: That's going to be so inspirational I know for a lot of readers because that story you described, exercising hard, eating right, doing all those things that should be leading to weight-loss, it doesn't work for a lot of people. I believe your story's so true that sleep is quite often that misunderstood or overlooked variable.

Debra: Yeah. Agreed. I guess one more thing that'll drive that home. This woman is 63. If she can do it, you can do it.

Dave: That's so cool. We talked about tracking diet, tracking protein intake, and then tracking sleep. I love even the idea of writing down what time of night do your eyes start to get heavy and if you go to bed at that time, what time will you wake up the next day, how did you sleep.

There's one other thing I wanted to ask just based on what Sandra wrote here. It sounds like she is doing a lot of exercise and you just talked about your story with Jennifer, her taking, gasp, two days off! What do you recommend for that balance between work and rest?

TEST AND FIND WHAT WORKS FOR YOU

Debra: Oh boy, that can be a tricky question Dave because it is so unique. I think the first thing I want to float out before we dive into that is that it is not an indication that you are wimpy or that you're deconditioned if you need more time off. Elite athletes vary in how much recovery they need. It's why they each have their own coach.

Some individuals just naturally recover better than others, but say your Olympic athlete may need two days between really intense workouts whereas another one might be able to go again the next day with just a single day of rest between. It really varies. You can't compare yourself to anyone else.

The rule of thumb is always "Test, don't guess."

First, if you're looking, Sandra for instance, at what you're doing now, take a look at your exercise schedule. Look at your Monday through Friday or Monday through Sunday and if you notice right now that it's not working, let's change it. If you're taking one day off between intense exercise, let's try two.

Now, on those recovery days, you can still move. We want you to be active, but rather than pay attention to maybe distance or minutes or heart rate, intensity or speed, you go outside, you go for a walk. It's a recovery walk, or it's yoga, or stretching. You can move, but in a less punishing way, a more friendly recovery way.

That's one way to look at. What we do know is that research says that as we age, adults who once got by with Monday-Wednesday-Friday workout schedules, which is so common, may not be able to do that as well anymore.

What Dave, you noticed, right, is that it takes a little bit longer to recover as we age. It might be that doing lifting on Monday and Thursday. This might make more sense for you, and you actually might get better results even though you're doing less resistance training.

Listen to your body on that. If you're still sore, if you feel like you're still partially recovering when you're about to start your next workout, take another day of recovery before you start again.

Dave: Yeah. What you said is so true. If it's not working then it's time to change. Our bodies are awesome at telling us what works and what doesn't work.

Debra: So true. It's just listening and backing off. I was, in fact, just writing a program and talked about how sometimes, instead of a seven-day workout week, which is what we're also used to from our school and work weeks, you might have to go with a nine-day workout schedule. You can lift weights on Monday, lift on Thursday, lift again on Sunday, which means you couldn't go again on Monday so you've got to wait again and start over.

Dave: You know what I love about the nine-day or a ten or eleven-day workout schedule? This would avoid everyone flooding the gym on Monday! Monday is so busy. Everyone goes to the gym on Monday.

Debra: I hear, "It's all about Dave." (laughs)

Dave: Yeah. Exactly. Jeez. (laughs)

Debra: I just can't emphasize enough that you need to listen to the signals that your body's sending you. I thoroughly believe you can be as good or better in the second 50 and as you get older. It's just that your strategy needs to change in order to help you do that.

Listen to the signals. If you're tired, you're sore, you're doing the right things but not getting the results that you think that you should, you need to take one variable and change it and test it.

Dave: I like the emphasis on one variable. Don't do too much too soon.

Debra: Right, because it will be hard to know what change was it that worked.

171

Dave: Debra, it was awesome having you as my guest today. Thanks so much.

Debra: Thank you. It's always fun to talk to you, Dave.

RESOURCES

Debra's Website: https://www.flippingfifty.com

Debra's book, *You've Still Got It, Girl!*: http://makeyourbodywork.com/still-got-it-girl

173

CHAPTER 11:

DOES FASTING REALLY WORK?

When's the last time you skipped a meal? What about skipping two meals in a row?

The thought of fasting, intentionally go without food for a predetermined length of time, seems pretty antiquated. It's a religious practice, not something you do to improve your health, right?

Actually, recent research has shown that fasting can help you effectively lose weight and keep it off. The practice is called *Intermittent Fasting*, and it's shown remarkable health benefits in many studies.

Still, Lori wasn't convinced:

> *"I'm hearing a lot about fasting, and how it can help people lose weight. What's your take, is this a healthy approach?"*

I'll admit that I like to eat, and I don't enjoy being hungry. The idea of fasting on a regular basis doesn't sound appealing, but if it works for improved health and weight management, then it might be worth considering.

MEET DR. JASON FUNG

Dr. Jason Fung is a nephrologist, a doctor specializing in work with the kidneys and related diseases. His extensive expertise in the areas of diabetes and obesity has made him a sought-after speaker and writer on these topics.

To help treat those dealing with diabetes and obesity, Dr. Fung has created the Intensive Dietary Management (IDM) Program and has written 2 national bestselling books, *The Obesity Code* and *The Complete Guide to Fasting*.

THE INTERVIEW

Dave: Hey, Doctor Fung, thank you so much for joining us in this interview today.

Jason: Thank you.

Dave: I'm excited to have you because I heard about you from some clients who are emailing me articles written about you. They had seen you or listened to you on CBC. At this point, I am very familiar with your work. I was wondering if you could fill in the readers who haven't heard about you before what it is you do? What do you specialize in? What are your latest contributions to health and fitness?

Jason: Sure, Dave. I'm a nephrologist—that's a kidney specialist—and I treat a lot of type two diabetes cases. I've been doing this for about fifteen years, now. The funny part about type two diabetes is most doctors in the healthcare system—in general—focus on drugs. What drugs to give, how much drugs to give. But the real problem is the weight, and everybody knows that.

Even patients know that. If you lose the weight, then diabetes goes away. Once diabetes goes away, you don't have to deal with diabetic problems, because you don't have them. In the end, everybody knows it's about the obesity problem, and that's how I became interested in treating the problem of obesity.

A DIETARY SOLUTION FOR A DIETARY PROBLEM

That's where I started a clinic called the *Intensive Dietary Management Program* (IDM), which focuses on using dietary manipulation to deal with the problem of obesity and type two diabetes. If you think about it, if you have a dietary problem, then you need a dietary solution.

You can't throw drugs at it because that's not going to work. It's like bringing a snorkel to a bicycle race. You've got the wrong idea. The problem was the dietitians, doctors, and everybody else was so focused on one thing: calories. We've been obsessed about calories for forty, fifty years. Nobody thought much outside of that.

The real problem is if you don't understand what causes obesity, you can't treat it. Nobody thinks of this problem much because they believe calories causes obesity. Too many calories. Calories in, calories out. But that idea is completely false. It's not simply calories because the different foods we eat have different metabolic effects on our body.

If you have refined carbohydrates, say cookies, and you have salad, they have different effects when you eat them. They're not the same at all. We can measure those results. It's very easy. We've known there are different effects for at least fifty, sixty years, so how can anyone say they are the same?

WHY A CALORIE IS NOT A CALORIE

When you think about the "a calorie is a calorie" idea, what you get are crazy ideas. For example, you can eat this plate of cookies, or you can eat this salad with grilled salmon, and they'll be equally fattening because they have the same number of calories.

Dave: Which is something proposed by—I don't mean to slam them—Weight Watchers. The premise behind getting points based on the calories in certain foods.

Jason: Yeah. Weight Watchers varies their points based on proprietary, but there are differences. I'm not familiar with it because I've never done Weight Watchers myself, but I do know people who have done it. A few years ago, there was a controversy. I think they were going to take away all points for fruits, or something.

Dave: Yeah.

Jason: The idea certain foods are more points than others reflects the notion certain foods are more fattening than others. Of course, everybody knows this is true. If you can eat sugar, it's more fattening than if you eat broccoli. They can be equal number of calories, but one is fattening, and one is not. That's the whole premise.

That is what I talk about in my book. Why this calorie idea is completely false and laying out where the logical traps are so you don't get caught in them. Then I explore what really causes obesity, which is essentially a hormonal imbalance, not a caloric one. Because hormones control everything in our bodies.

They tell us how to grow—puberty—they tell us how much metabolism they control. Hormones control everything in our body. Our body weight is the same. We all assume that it's completely unregulated, that our body weight is entirely unregulated. No system in the body is completely unregulated. We have very powerful systems to tell us when we should eat, and when we should not eat.

That's the whole idea, and we have to understand what causes it. If we understand hormones—the main ones here are insulin and cortisol—is the problem, then we have to figure out how we're going to lower insulin if that's what the problem is.

Dave: Your book is called *The Obesity Code* and in the *Resources* section of this chapter I'll link directly out to it for the readers. Can you explain how insulin and cortisol work together, or work in hand to control weight?

HOW INSULIN AND CORTISOL WORK

Jason: Yeah. Insulin is the primary hormone involved when we eat. When we eat, insulin goes up, and that tells our body to store some of that food energy, like sugar—which is glycogen—and fat. That's normal.

If you eat a big meal, then you store some of that energy in your body as sugar and fat. When you don't eat, or when you fast, insulin levels fall, and it tells our body to pull some of that food energy back out. This process is an entirely normal situation.

If you have a situation where insulin levels are abnormally high, then our bodies are going to store fat. That's its normal job. It's just we have too much of it.

Cortisol is more complicated. It's known as the stress hormone. But the mechanism is slightly different. It releases a lot of glucose and may play a role in raising insulin in the long-term.

The idea here is a hormonal imbalance. There's nothing intrinsically wrong with insulin; it's just the disease is too much insulin. Therefore, we have to figure out how we're going to reduce it. For example, certain foods stimulate insulin a lot, and other foods hardly stimulate it at all.

Therefore, if you're trying to reduce the insulin, you want to eat less food that stimulates a lot of insulin. Those are the refined carbohydrates, sugars, refined grains, and flour. I think people know this already. You're not supposed to eat white sugar or white bread if you want to try to lose weight. People have started to get back to this idea.

DIETARY FAT: THE LEAST FATTENING FOOD

Dave: Ten years ago, it was all about the low-fat foods, which may be even more processed foods than we eat now.

Jason: Exactly. The entire landscape of dietary fat, especially from about fifteen years ago, has changed. Back then it was all about low fat. Now, we see people talking about healthy fats. Dietary fat is one of the three major macronutrients. And of carbohydrates, protein, and fat, it stimulates insulin the least.

It is actually the least fattening. As before, we always thought, if you eat a lot of fat, you're going to get fat. It's not true because it doesn't stimulate insulin. And this is the whole difference between calories and hormones because fat is very high in calories, but it doesn't stimulate insulin much. Dietary fat has completely come around.

A lot of the research helps us realize there's no link between fat and heart disease, which was the major problem. Now, all the studies show there's no problem. Now we're at the point where olive oil and avocados—high-fat foods—are super foods. Fifteen years ago, people would say, "Oh, my God, you're eating an avocado?"

179

But now everybody says you should eat more avocado. The same with nuts, like macadamia nuts. They're very high in fat, and fifteen years ago it was like, "Oh, my God, you can't eat those nuts, there's so much fat in there." Now, it's like, "Oh, you should eat more nuts."

The research bares that out. People who eat more nuts have less heart disease. We know those who eat lots of olive oil—the Mediterranean Diet—have also shown less heart disease. The Mediterranean Diet is a higher fat diet because it adds all olive oil and nuts.

Dave: Yeah. It's good to hear you say that. I know there is confusion about if this diet works. It's good to hear the latest and greatest from a scientific perspective: this is how your body actually responds to these types of foods.

How to Choose Natural Foods

Jason: Yeah. I hate the "latest and greatest." I think you should go to the oldest, the tried and true. Because those are the treatments that have withstood the test of time. What we talked about, and in my book, is eating natural foods.

Eat food that's natural, and grows from the ground. That includes carbohydrates, unprocessed carbohydrates, fat, and proteins.

What you don't want to eat is a box of Lucky Charms, or something, because that doesn't grow from the earth. You don't have to worry if you are eating a lot of natural vegetables.

The grains are different because they are highly processed. Vegetable oils, although they're fats, are highly processed fats. Try to avoid those highly processed foods. For instance, manufacturers take a wheat berry and strip away everything except the carbohydrate.

Before you had a whole food, which had carbohydrate, protein, and fat. Now, you take away all that, and you only have the carbohydrates, so the balance is completely thrown off.

Our bodies are supposed to have this balance. We can process normal, natural foods, but we cannot process refined ultra-processed foods, and that's the real problem we have today.

Dave: Yeah. You threw out the example of Lucky Charms, and I think most people would look at a bowl of Lucky Charms, and realize that's not a healthy food.

When you look at foods marketed as being healthy—and I'll use bread as an example—you can see all kinds of loaves of bread on the shelf. They have all sorts of health claims on them, and an unaware consumer might look at that and think, "Hey, this says it's low in fat, high in fiber, and a source of protein. Therefore, it must be healthy. But like you said, it's ultra-processed.

Jason: Yeah. The real problem is people make a lot of health points about different things, whether it's protein, fat, carbs, or fiber. But you can't simply take fiber, stick it into some processed foods, and say it's healthy for you.

In the end, you have to go with natural foods, so you don't have to worry about what your percentages. Sometimes people get hung up with percentage fat, percentage carbohydrate, and everything else.

If you go back and look at traditional societies, for example, some ate eighty, ninety percent carbohydrates. Okinawans, for instance, eat a lot of sweet potatoes, and they were some of the healthiest people on earth.

This is traditional. Now, of course, they've been westernized. Sweet potatoes have kind of gone downhill. You also have people like the Inuit who eat whale blubber and seal fat, so practically all protein and fat. You go from one extreme to the other, and yet, in both societies, there is virtually no obesity, and no type two diabetes.

This tells us we don't have to focus so closely on these macro-nutrients, instead on processing. One of the points I make in my book toxicity lies in the processing, rather than the foods itself.

Dave: The comparison between macronutrient makeup and different people groups around the world is interesting. It sounds like the Weston Price metabolic typing diet or philosophy. The idea there isn't a one-size-fits-all solution, but what is tried and true examples of what can work.

Jason: Exactly. I always find it funny, regarding new super foods, when somebody says, "Oh, you should eat this dairy or quinoa." They're fine foods, but we can do fine without them.

It always strikes me as slightly ridiculous when somebody comes out with something like raspberry ketones, or green coffee. I think, "Okay, in the past five thousand years of human history, you suddenly found food that every single one of the billions of people in the world has missed. And you, today, think this is going to make everything all right."

That's ridiculous. All foods that are natural can be super foods. People survived on all kinds of diets and did well. Like Weston Price, he said, "You can look at all different places in the world, and have different diets, and still do well, what's the common thread? They are not processed." They're not going through a factory and then coming out into our mouths. They're naturally unprocessed foods.

WHAT WORKED IN THE PAST STILL WORKS TODAY

My bias is to look at things that have been done for thousands of years. If they've been done for thousands of years, then they're likely fairly beneficial. Intermittent fasting is a perfect example. I was reading this the other day, it's the latest diet craze, and I'm thinking, "Seriously?"

People have been fasting for at least five thousand years, minimum. You're calling it the latest diet craze. Why don't you call bowel movements the latest diet craze? That's ridiculous. I think you have to look back at what has worked in the past and give it a fair chance.

Why do we believe that we're so much smarter today? Because we figured out that fasting isn't bad for you when people have been doing it for thousands of years? It's part of every major religion in the world. These people who preach fasting, like if you go to church, people talk about forty days of lent. People talk about fasting, all the time.

The priest is not trying to kill off all his parishioners. They're doing it because intermittent fasting is uniquely and deeply healthy. It's a way to staying well. It's a way to clean your body of all the junk you've accumulated over the last year. It's not going to kill you. Because if those religious leaders were going to kill off all the parishioners, then they wouldn't have anybody to lead.

Dave: It's bad for business.

Jason: Exactly. It's ridiculous to call it a diet craze. That's crazy.

Dave: I am glad you brought that up, because the question I wanted to address was from Lori, and she was asking about following an intermittent fasting diet plan. It's certainly been popularized within the last two, three years.

That's what I want to get down to because you talk about—in your book—using fasting as a mechanism to balance your hormones. I was wondering if you could talk about that from a practical standpoint. How could people start fasting? Why does it work? What should they be doing?

FASTING TO BALANCE YOUR HORMONES

Jason: Fasting is the flip side of eating. Whenever you're not eating, you are fasting. Technically, that's all it is. What we're saying is you need to balance eating and fasting. If you eat from 7 am, to 7 pm, that's 12 hours of eating, and from 7 pm to 7 am, that's 12 hours of fasting, now they're balanced.

If you eat from the minute you get up, to the minute you go to sleep, your metabolism is dominated by the feeding phase, which is insulin dominant, and you have very little of the fasting, which is insulin deficient. You are just giving your body the signal—the insulin—to store fat all the time. And you wonder why you are not losing weight.

It seems obvious now, doesn't it? If you've been way too far on the high insulin side, then you need to balance it. The way to do that is to lower it. Fasting is one way of bringing your insulin levels down. It doesn't mean you fast for 40 days and 40 nights.

You can do it for 12 hours, 16 hours, 24 hours, or whatever you'd like. There are no rules on it, and there's nothing unnatural about this situation. It's simply a period where you let your body burn off the energy you have stored. The energy from last night's dinner, from yesterday's lunch, you want to burn it off, so you fast, so your body has time to burn it off. That's it.

WE FAST ALL THE TIME!

Dave: I like your point: there isn't a set time period. I can remember as a teenager, a religious-based event, where all these teenagers would get together and fast for twenty-four hours, raising money for a certain charity.

I remember thinking, "There is no way I could do a fast!" But then someone pointed out I fast every single night for at least twelve, maybe sixteen hours. It seems so much more surmountable when you realize you fast all the time.

Jason: Exactly. Even our word, "breakfast." It's the meal that breaks your fast, which means you have to fast. It's a part of everyday life. What it means intrinsically is it has to be part of daily life. Whether it's 12 hours, if you don't eat from 7 the night before until 7, that's twelve hours of fasting right there.

Dave: I know people readers are thinking, "Well, tell me exactly what I need to do to start incorporating an official intermittent fasting diet plan into my life." And, from our conversation, it sounds like there is no one size fits all. But for someone who wants to extend their fasting period, what would you suggest? Should they do it on a weekly basis? Should they do it every couple days? How much should they extend that fasting period by?

TOP INTERMITTENT FASTING DIET PLANS YOU CAN FOLLOW

Jason: There are different regimens, for example, a popular one is to fast 16 hours and balance it with 8 hours of eating. That would mean eating, for example, from 11 am to 7 pm and fasting the rest of the time.

Dave: That being on an ongoing basis?

Jason: Yeah. You can do that every day. You could extend and do a 24 hour fast. So, you go from dinner, skip breakfast and lunch, and go to dinner again. You might not need to do that every day, although some people do.

You might do it twice a week, but for example, I say, three times a week. You can do anything in between, or you can go above that. Although, once you start going longer and longer, you have to be careful, regarding medications and different things.

Watch out for side effects, but if you stick to the twenty-four hours, most people find it very doable, especially on a workday. We have a phobia of skipping breakfast. It's ridiculous because most people are not that hungry in the morning. If you look at studies of circadian rhythms, the lowest point in hunger you will ever have is about 8 am.

This is the point where people say, "You need to shove something in your mouth, right now." But if you are not hungry, shoving something in your mouth is not a winning strategy for weight-loss. Isn't that bloody obvious? Not to most people and many dietitians. Many conventional advice givers, say, "Shove something in your mouth. I don't care if you're not hungry."

The problem is that it goes against what your body is telling you. Your body is saying, "You are not hungry, you don't need to eat buddy." But you eat something regardless. You don't have to worry about that because you're not going to shut down.

THE MYTH OF A STARVATION MODE

The idea of starvation mode doesn't happen during fasting. What's mildly ironic about this myth, which says your metabolism will start to shut down, and therefore you're not going to burn as many calories. It's easier to regain weight.

The funny part is, when you cut calories, your body does go into starvation mode. When you fast, it doesn't. Your body switches fuel sources. It's not shutting down; it turns from burning food to burning fat which is just stored food. It doesn't shut down, and studies bare that. Fat is nothing more than stored food energy. That's what it's there for, for you to eat when you have nothing to eat. It's not there for looks.

185

If you are eating all the time, your body has no reason to go into its fat stores. Why would it? It doesn't make any sense. Then, you just keep burning food energy and you wonder why you can't lose weight.

Dave: I like that you've shown the difference between going into starvation mode by eating a reduced calorie diet, perpetually, versus following an intermittent fasting diet plan and reducing your calories a day a week, or two days a week.

That's hard for people to get in their minds. They've heard so much about fasting in the media and think, "I can't fast because my metabolism will shut down." But you're definitively saying, that's not true.

Jason: Yeah. That's not true. A study shows if you measure your metabolic rate after four days of continuous fasting and compare it to your rate at the beginning of the four days, your metabolic rate is about thirteen percent higher than when you started.

Dave: Wow.

Jason: Your body is not shutting down, it's revving up. This makes sense if you're a cave man and you have nothing to eat. You don't start shutting down. Instead, the body switches fuel sources and it gives you extra energy to go out and find something to eat.

If you're weak, you'll just curl up and die, because it's a vicious cycle. You get weaker if you don't find food, and when you get even weaker, you can't find food. It's a viscous cycle.

But we would not be sitting here talking if our bodies worked like that. Our bodies aren't stupid. What our body does is say, "You've stored food energy away, it's right there, let's take it out, and let me give you a little boost of adrenaline. Now, go out and find me some food." So, you do.

Dave: It's interesting, that's an excellent way to look at it. Anyone who has practiced fasting before experientially will know that's true. Maybe the first or second meal of the day, when you are used to eating habitually, you might feel a little bit hungry. But I would argue that's more of a psychological construct than a

186

physiological one. And then afterward, once you get through it, generally, there is plenty of energy.

Jason: There's a lot. People are worried they're not going to have any energy. Think about the last time you had a large Thanksgiving meal, immediately after, were you super energetic, or were you in a food coma lying on the couch watching football?

Dave: Yeah.

Jason: You didn't have any energy because the blood is digesting your food. On the other hand, think about when you see somebody hungry for something, hungry for power, hungry for this.

Does that mean you're lying on the couch in the fetal position? I don't think so. When you're hungry for something, it means you're hyped up, and ready to go. When you fast, your body is not shutting down at all. You're poised and ready for action.

Dave: Thank you for all this wisdom Doctor Fung. Now, your book, *The Obesity Code*, I know readers are interested in checking it out. Where's the best place they can find it?

Jason: You can find it at Amazon and most bookstores will have it. For more information, you could go to my website, which is www.intensivedietarymanagement.com. That's the program we run, the Intensive Dietary Management Program. We have a weekly blog and there are links to all of our videos.

Dave: Perfect. Doctor Fung, thanks again, for taking the time for this interview today, and sharing your wisdom. I really appreciate it.

Jason: Thank you.

RESOURCES

Dr. Fung's Website: https://intensivedietarymanagement.com

Dr. Fung's Book: http://makeyourbodywork.com/jf-obesity-code

Metabolic Typing Diet Book (Influenced by Weston Price's Work):
http://makeyourbodywork.com//jf-metabolic-typing

CHAPTER 12:

DOES YOUR EXERCISE HELP OR HURT?

So far we've talked a lot about mindset, habit building, nutrition, and many other factors that contribute to your ability to take control of your health and your weight, but we've only briefly discussed exercise.

Isn't exercise a critical component of weight-loss? And if it is, why do so many people who exercise still struggle with their weight?

Joy found herself in that position. She exercises, but her body doesn't change the ways she'd like:

> *"I feel like I'm lucky because I actually love to exercise. I go to the gym every day to do cardio, weights, classes, and almost always look forward to it. But I still carry a little extra weight around my waist and in my butt.*
>
> *Sometimes I wonder if I'm exercising too much, what do you think? I really just want to be healthy but would love to tone up, too."*

While all physical activity is great, not all exercise is created equal. The right type of exercise can greatly increase your body's ability to shed fat. The wrong exercise can lead you into a plateau, or worse, increased fat storage.

MEET LAURA JACKSON

 Laura Jackson is a certified personal trainer and is the founder of *Fit Chicks*, an exercise company that serves women across Canada.

In addition to helping thousands of women get in shape through her fitness programming, Laura makes appearances on TV and writes many published articles about effective exercise. She also helps train other fitness professionals through her Fit Chicks Academy and is the host of the *Fit Chicks Chat* podcast.

THE INTERVIEW

Dave: Hey, Laura. Thanks so much for joining us today.

Laura: Hi, I'm pumped to be here!

Dave: Yeah, I'm excited. So, we met at a fitness conference a couple of weeks ago, and as soon as I learned about your business, I knew I wanted to interview you. I appreciate you taking the time.

Laura: That's awesome. I've heard about you, too. I know you are one of the top fitness professionals in Canada, congratulations.

Dave: Ha - Thanks. Old news way back in 2013.

Laura: Yeah, but I've still heard of you in the circle, so I was like "Oh! I'd love to be interviewed by you."

Dave: That's great. Well, maybe you can start off by telling the readers about your business and what your specialties are, and how you got into the whole fitness world.

Laura: Yeah, for sure. So, I am co-founder of Fit Chicks, which is Canada's largest women-only fitness company. We mainly do boot camps, so we started with women-only boot camps in Toronto. Our approach was providing challenging fitness, but fitness that's inclusive to all levels of fitness.

It took off and started expanding. Now we have over twenty locations across Canada. We also have fitness retreats, and we have a DVD line. We also just started providing online certifications for other fitness professionals with our Fit Chicks Academy. So, we have a program called the Fitness and Nutrition Expert Program, and our next one launches in April.

Dave: You are busy, wow. I don't know how you do all that.

Laura: We do a lot of different stuff, but I just love health, fitness, wellness, and female empowerment all wrapped into one. I think there's such a need for it. I'm all about giving back and getting involved in the community as much as I can.

MORE EXERCISE FOR BETTER RESULTS?

Dave: That's awesome. When you and I were chatting by email about what topic to cover, I got this question from Joy, and I think it lends itself so well to your expertise.

In summary, Joy says she's going to the gym every day: she lifts weights, goes to classes, and all this stuff. But she's still not getting the results she's looking for. She finds she still has some weight around her waist and butt. Do you experience this when you work with your clients at all? Maybe clients who over-exercise?

Laura: Yeah, when you sent me this question, I thought, "This is a question I get a lot." I think we're always in this mentality of more is better, and it's not. Smarter is better; that's the way that I approach things.

So, with this question, I took a step back, because there are many factors in play preventing you from reaching your goals when you're exercising—especially for women. I know she was saying she's at the gym every day doing cardio, weights, and classes.

Immediately, I think of looking at other factors, besides just her going to the gym. Especially for women, there are so many other things that play into reaching your goals. Whether it's weight-loss, muscle building, or maintenance, just hitting the gym won't get you there.

I know she's doing cardio, weights, and classes every day, which is a lot. But, I'd like to know, how many days of cardio versus how many days of weights is she doing? Because that's massive and I'll get more into that in a moment. I also would love to know what her nutrition is like because you cannot out train a bad diet, which we all know.

Dave: Thank you for reinforcing that, very true.

Laura: In these cases, often the person isn't necessarily eating poorly. When we think of a bad diet, we think of junk food or processed foods. But it's more about how much you are eating regarding your macronutrient balance, which are your proteins, carbohydrates, and fats.

For example, if she's going to the gym every single day but she's eating a super carb-heavy diet with little protein, she's not going to build muscle—that's going to help her burn more—because muscle is metabolically active. It's going to be counterproductive.

Dave: Laura, let me jump in there because you're covering a lot of relevant topics and I want to break these down for the readers. First of all, you talked about if you could talk to Joy you would want to know the breakdown of her workouts, like what they consist of. For someone who is trying to lose weight and feels like they're stuck, what do you recommend?

DON'T BE AFRAID TO LIFT WEIGHTS

Laura: For someone who is like Joy, because she obviously is more advanced, I would recommend her to focus more on her strength training. Instead of doing cardio, weights, and the classes, focus on four to five days a week of going heavier with the weights. Lifting—not to complete failure because we want her to walk the next day—where those last couple reps are a real struggle.

Dave: Maybe you can explain to readers who aren't familiar with that term. What does it mean to exercise to failure?

Laura: Well, it means a one-rep max; you can only do one. It's so heavy you can only do one. Or, if you're training to failure, exercising until you reach the last rep you cannot physically do.

Dave: So, you push yourself to the point where your muscles start to fail, and they can't contract any longer.

Laura: Yeah, and the whole purpose of doing that is to break down your muscle, so it will rebuild itself.

Dave: It's interesting you brought up going straight to weight training. This is very unintentional, but I've had a string of guests and probably four or five—all women—have said the same thing: ladies, if you want to lose weight you got to start hitting the weights, and don't be afraid to increase the amount of weight you're lifting. And it sounds like you're on the same page.

Laura: Oh, completely. A lot of times women are looking for these popular curves like the Kim Kardashians, even though—let's be real—I don't know if those are fully worked for. If you're lifting weights, you're going to reshape your body composition.

I say to my clients not to worry about the weight on the scale because you can be a tight, strong size four and weigh the same as a size eight who doesn't have as much muscle tone. Don't focus on the number, focus on different measurables like performance measurables, the way your clothes fit, and the way your body shape starts to change.

Dave: I like that you point out—straight from Joy's message—she's probably a more advanced exerciser. Purely based on that she exercises a ton and does quite a variety.

So, for someone like her, maybe doing four or five strength training sessions would be great. What about someone who typically goes to the gym and is on the treadmill, or elliptical, and that's all she is doing. Does she jump in and do four sessions of strength training a week?

Laura: I would say start with three and see how you feel, then go to four or five. Also, start to learn proper form. I think a lot of people jump in too fast. They do four or five days a week and then injure themselves, which sets you back way further. Also, it's discouraging. I would say start off with three.

Dave: I think that's fair. Giving yourself at least a day of rest in between each session.

How Exercise Impacts Cortisol Levels

Laura: Yeah. I'm not big on cardio, but I think cardio has its place. I believe, especially for women, we have a mentality of being cardio bunnies. Another thing women overlook is hormones. We do cardio so much, but there's so much research coming out now, showing it's hard on our bodies.

It elevates what's called cortisol, which is your fight or flight reaction when you get stressed about something. You want to either run for the hills or go Rocky on someone and knock them out. It is also responsible for holding on to fat, especially around the waist. Which Joy mentioned as well.

If you're overtraining, you're going to increase cortisol levels. If you're training for too long, you're going to increase cortisol levels. And if you are not managing your lifestyle outside of working out, like stress management, you're going to elevate your cortisol levels, too.

Find your sweet spot and sometimes it requires taking a step back. Maybe taking a break from the gym and seeing how your body reacts to that, then coming back into it with a different approach. More strength, less cardio and go from there.

Dave: What you just said is so wise. I assume you can relate to this, but let me know. One thing I've encountered clients with is saying, "Okay, I'm only going to do cardio two to three times a week, and I'm going to focus on strength training."

But they have this idea strength training is a super high-intensity interval training, or doing classes where they are lifting weights. So, they think that's strength training. But in reality, their heart rate is flying for the entire class or session, and it's almost like doing another session of cardio.

Laura: Completely. Our Fit Chicks boot camp we do, they're all based on high-intensity interval training. They are an hour long, but the high-intensity cardio parts are much shorter to complement longer body weight and weight training resistance. You're getting the balance of both, but you're not burning at this crazy high level throughout the entire class where your body is doing more harm than good.

Dave: A hundred percent. Again, I'm glad you said that. When I read Joy's message, the first thing I thought was picturing her in step class, and all these high aerobic classes, plus all the cardio she's doing. Her workouts may almost be all cardio. Solely cardio, potentially.

Laura: Exactly. I think there's still a lot of women who are so afraid of getting bulky, and that's why they step away from thinking about picking up the heavier weights. I always tell my clients, "You have to think of it as your muscles are like a stove."

You want the stove to burn, so it needs fuel. Because muscles metabolically active, it's the best deal ever. If you build more muscle, then you get to burn more calories sitting around and doing nothing. Who doesn't want that?

Dave: I love that quote, it is the best deal ever. Muscle is the best deal ever, I agree.

Laura: Totally! Put the work in the gym and then let your body rest and build. Then it turns into a fat-burning machine. You're not going to get bulky; we don't have the hormones to get bulky. Unless you're taking drugs—as a female—you're not going to suddenly turn into Arnold Schwarzenegger if you pick up a fifteen-pound weight.

Dave: I was talking to a guest about our workout plans, and I was saying how I lift really heavy weights because I was trying to bulk up. I had a female client email me who said, "Hey, Dave, you have me lifting heavy weights. Shouldn't I be worried about bulking up like you're trying to do?"

Exactly your message, I said, "A — Our hormones are completely different. And B — I'm eating four to five thousand calories a day right now," and I don't think most women are doing that.

Laura: Exactly. I've done fitness competitions as well, which is baby bodybuilding, and whole other conversation. I'm tall at 5'10", and I'm basically a *mesomorph*. I gain muscle easily, and I can gain fat easily as well. But I'm tall, so to put on noticeable muscle takes a lot of work for me. It takes a lot of heavy lifting, eating, and eating the right foods. I was eating a lot of protein at nutrient-timed intervals so my body could effectively use that food to build the muscle.

Dave: Yeah, and we'll get into that. I would like to ask you about diet in just a second. On the exercise piece, your message has been: lift more weights, start at maybe three sessions a week, work your way up to four or five, reduce the amount of cardio, allow your body's hormones to adjust, and allow your body to start building calorie-burning material, muscle.

But what about for someone—and I think Joy is in this spot too—who says, "Okay, I'll go and do the weights, but I can't give up my cardio. It feels wrong to give up my cardio." Do you ever deal with clients like that? It's like a mental switch they just can't flip.

SHORT AND SWEET CARDIO SESSIONS

Laura: Yeah, a lot. Like I said before, I do think cardio has its place. Cardiovascular training is about having a healthy heart. I believe we need to shift our mentality of cardio from thinking we need to do this forty-five-minute step class or an hour on the elliptical trainer—which I think is the most useless machine. I'm sorry to whoever created it.

Dave: Ha!

Laura: I know, but it's the most unnatural motion. Anyways, I think it's shifting your thoughts around cardio. I do build in cardio for some of them depending on their goals. If it's fat-loss, I might give them two to three days a week.

But, I do it briefly and after their weights. They have to do their weights first, so they have maximum energy for their lifts. Then I might do eight minutes of high-intensity intervals following their workout. But I try to keep them in the gym for no longer than forty-five minutes because, after forty-five minutes, their cortisol level can spike.

If they have a longer weight-training day, then maybe I'll tell them to do cardio at another time during the day or on a different day. It will still be short, perhaps eight to twelve minutes.

Dave: Okay, great. That's practical for all of the women—and maybe men— reading. Short workouts—forty-five minutes or less—and if you're going to tack on cardio, put it after your weight training session.

One thing I want to add is I've read some studies that talk about the diminishing returns of working out longer. Forty-five minutes was the sweet spot where your body is experiencing those adaptations. But after the forty-five-minute point, the gains you receive drastically decrease for the amount of effort and time you're putting in.

HOW YOUR BODY HOLDS ON TO WEIGHT

Laura: Working out is putting your body in a state of stress, although there are positive benefits. I had a client before who was a marathon runner. You would think after running three hours, five hours, or whatever it was, you would lose weight.

But her body did the exact opposite. She would go into marathon season and be up around thirteen pounds because her body was in a state of stress. Plus, her hormones were all over the map. Her cortisol is thinking something bad is going to happen, and it has to hold on to every pound it can.

Our body wants to be healthy in the state of homeostasis, and it does its best keep what you need, thinking there's an attack coming. So, your body naturally holds on to fat. It was crazy to see because you would think from the amount of output she would drop weight like crazy, but it was the opposite.

Dave: That's so valuable. Readers, think about the point Laura just made. You can be exercising so hard, putting in so many hours a week, but if your hormones are out of whack and you're not caring for your body, you will not get the results you're looking for.

THE ROLE OF TOXINS AND WEIGHT GAIN

Laura: Hormones are one of my passions right now; I'm really into the hormonal side of health. I think it's overlooked. Also, we're getting exposed to lots of toxins. It's said we're exposed to over thirty toxins before we eat breakfast.

Dave: Wow.

Laura: What happens, and how it applies to weight-loss and health, is these toxins build up in your body and they interfere with your natural hormonal processes. The hormones that influence your body composition. These are things like thyroid function, testosterone, estrogen, and insulin.

Toxins go into your body, go haywire, and try to mimic your hormones. Studies are showing one of the reasons why a lot of people are gaining weight so rapidly is because of toxins doing all these crazy things to our bodies.

Dave: So, for someone like Joy, someone who is stuck, they're exercising like they think they should but still not seeing results. What can they do diet-wise to see progress but also to avoid exposure to some of those toxins you referenced?

THE "COMPLETE AND 3" RULE

Laura: The first thing I always say to my clients is to go as un-packaged and unprocessed as possible. Buying foods without labels, things like vegetables, meat, fruit, and whole grains. All the foods with no need for a nutrition label because they're natural foods.

Then, I follow with what I call the *Complete and 3 Rule* because I think it's an easy thing to have in your back pocket. Every time you have a meal, you ensure it includes three things: protein, fiber, and a healthy fat. Whether you're at an event for work, or you're traveling, you know to avoid packaged and processed food.

From there, make sure your meal includes a protein, fiber, and fat, which balances your blood sugar, keeps your insulin levels from spiking, and prevents weight gain.

Dave: I love that, it's very practical and easy to remember. Can you just speak quickly on fiber? What do you recommend when people are looking for the fiber component?

Laura: Fiber is vital, and we're seeing such low levels of fiber consumption now because of the increase in packaged and processed foods. I would say between twenty-five to forty grams. If you're someone who hasn't been eating a lot of fiber, start with twenty-five and up your water intake, or you might be a little backed up. I personally always try to stay around the thirty-five to forty for myself.

Dave: That's per day?

Laura: Yeah, and it's easy when you're adding in things. Like a cup of raspberries has nine grams of fiber. You don't think of raspberries as fiber, but if you put a cup in your smoothie, that's nine grams right there. It adds up quickly.

Dave: Again, I liked how you emphasize that first and foremost, people need to move away from packaged or processed goods, especially when you talk about fiber. So many products are labeled as being high-fiber because people know fiber is good for them. But if people start looking at their meal with this complete and three method and think, "I need fiber, I'm going to grab small bran." That's defeating the whole purpose.

Laura: I'm also a holistic nutritionist. I focus on the health properties you're getting from food. Usually, something packaged with high fiber is also highly inflammatory and high in gluten—which a lot of us have reactions to now because wheat is not the same as it used to be. Many other things factor in too, so it's always best to go with Mother Nature. She's the best chef out there. Real whole foods are the way to go.

Dave: Great message. For the readers, if they wanted to learn more about you, your philosophies, what you do, where's the best place they can connect with you?

Laura: Head on over to our website, FitChicks.ca. We've got a ton of information on not only all of our classes and what we offer, but also our amazing blog that has free workouts, awesome recipes, and tips in general on wellness.

Dave: I was just looking at your blog, and it's awesome. Again, a very holistic approach I would highly recommend to any of the readers.

Laura: Well, thank you.

RESOURCES

Laura's Website: http://www.fitchicks.ca

CHAPTER 13:

IS SLEEP YOUR MISSING INGREDIENT?

I love sleep. When I hear from people who can "function" on 5 hours per night, I just can't relate.

What about you? How much sleep do you need to function? And, perhaps a more important question: how much sleep do you need to *thrive*?

Sleep is perhaps the most overlooked variable in the fat-loss equation. It seems optional, or nice to have. But, just how much is your sleep (or lack thereof) holding back your health and even causing you to pack on unwanted pounds? Sarah wanted to know:

> *"Hi, Dave. I've never been much of a sleeper. Ever since my 20s, I've always averaged maybe five or six hours of sleep per night, and it seems to work for me. I know that we're supposed to get eight hours, but I don't feel like I need it.*
>
> *At the same time, I do wonder if my lack of sleep could be damaging in some ways that I don't notice. If I feel good with five hours of sleep, do I really need more? If so, how do I force my body to sleep longer?"*

While Sarah doesn't ask specifically about the relationship between sleep and weight-loss, we know that the two are linked. To reach your optimal weight, you need to reach your optimal sleep and, as you're about to learn, your optimal sleep is likely different from what you might think.

MEET DR. MICHAEL BREUS

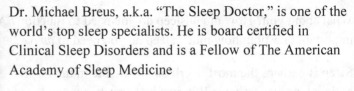

Dr. Michael Breus, a.k.a. "The Sleep Doctor," is one of the world's top sleep specialists. He is board certified in Clinical Sleep Disorders and is a Fellow of The American Academy of Sleep Medicine

For more than 16 years, Dr. Breus has been in practice, helping people find their optimal sleep rhythms. He has appeared on the "Dr. Oz" TV show 36 times and has authored many popular books and published articles.

His latest book, *The Power of When*, teaches how you can discover the best time to do everything–from drinking your coffee to having sex or going for a run–according to your body's sleep chronotype.

THE INTERVIEW

Dave: Hi, Dr. Breus. Thanks so much for joining me for this interview.

Dr. Breus: Thanks, Dave. I'm excited to be here.

Dave: Now, you are known as "The Sleep Doctor." Maybe we could talk a little bit about that. How did you get that name?

Dr. Breus: Sure. How did I end up with that moniker? I have a PhD in clinical psychology, and I'm board certified in clinical sleep disorders. I'm an actively practicing sleep specialist. I took the medical specialty board without going to medical school and passed. I'm one of only 160 people who've ever done that. I've been practicing sleep medicine in conjunction with my physician partners for my entire career, all 16 years. I treat things like apnea and narcolepsy. My specialty, as it turns out, is insomnia.

Dave: I'm really excited to have you here for this interview. I have a whole backlog of questions from people who have been asking about sleep. I usually don't run a question until I find the perfect expert to address the topic. When you and I got connected, I thought, "Finally, we can talk about this, and I've got someone who knows what they're talking about."

Dr. Breus: Absolutely.

Dave: Can you tell me a little bit about your personal story? What was it that got you interested in this particular line of work?

Dr. Breus: It was rather serendipitous. I was doing my residency training, and there were rotations you could take. You could take one in addiction, in PTSD, or sports psychology. There was also a six-month rotation in sleep. I just thought, "Well, that sounds cool. I don't know a lot about it." This was 17 years ago, actually longer. I said, "I'll give it a shot." By the third day, I absolutely fell in love with clinical sleep medicine.

As a clinical psychologist, it can take weeks, months, even years to see treatment gains for people who have depression, or anxiety, or things like that. What I discovered with sleep is, I can literally change somebody's life in 24 to 48 hours. It's amazing how quickly people who have sleep issues respond to my therapies and my treatment, especially on the insomnia and apnea side.

Dave: Awesome. I was reading a statement, a really powerful statement, on your website earlier today. It says, "There's virtually no skill, task or function, no physiological process, no emotion or relationship that isn't affected by sleep." Even just going with that statement, everyone who's reading this book, if your sleep isn't perfect, we're hopefully going to change your life a little bit with what we talk about today.

Now, Sarah wrote to me. I've gotten a lot of questions about sleep, but I think hers wraps up a lot of the ideas into one question. She says ever since her adult life began, she averages five or six hours of sleep and she's "getting by." But she also knows there's a rule of thumb saying you're supposed to get eight hours of sleep.

She's wondering what could be happening to her body because of that lack of sleep and the fact she doesn't feel like she can sleep any longer. How can she change that, or should she be changing that? Let's start off with this question. What do you see with the patients or the clients you work with that are like Sarah, and chronically sleep five or six hours a night?

Dr. Breus: First of all, I want to dispel a myth that's out there. The myth is eight hours: very few people need exactly eight hours of sleep. That's something that the media hooked up on 10, 15 years ago. It's been pounding this idea into the pavement. The truth of the matter is it's not very accurate. Everybody has their own different sleep need.

As an example, I'm a six-and-a-half hour sleeper. I have been almost my entire life. My wife, she needs more, like eight or eight-and-a-half. What's fascinating here is you have to figure out what your individual sleep need is. Once you know that, there's a much better opportunity to have an achievable goal. So that's number one.

Dave: Can I stop you right there?

Dr. Breus: Sure.

Dave: How do you determine that?

HOW TO DETERMINE YOUR IDEAL SLEEP TIME

Dr. Breus: I do a little experiment. I teach people how to figure out what their bedtime is. I'm about to release a course, an online course, where people can learn more about their sleep and change their level of sleep regarding insomnia and things of that nature. Let me give everybody the quick preview of how to determine what your bedtime is.

Most people have a socially determined wake-up time because of work, or kids, or school, or something like that. And, we know that the average sleep cycle is approximately 90 minutes long. We also know that the average person has approximately five of those sleep cycles.

Now there can be variations here and there, but let's use those numbers just to make the math simple. Five times 90 is 450, divided by 60, is seven-and-a-half. If you wake up at 6:30, as an example, and you go back seven-and-a-half hours, that's 11 o'clock. That is your bedtime. Does that make sense?

Dave: Yeah, it does, but then that standardizes it for everyone.

Dr. Breus: That's only part one.

Dave: Sorry. I'm jumping ahead.

Dr. Breus: No, it's all good. Let me tell you about part two. If people start going to bed at 11, and they happen to wake up at 6:30, what they should find is that they're waking up either just after their alarm or maybe even before their alarm. Let's say that you go to bed at 11, and you wake up at six. Well, then you know that you only need seven hours, and so you can make your bedtime 11:30. You can fiddle around with it.

Dave: How long would you get someone to do this? If I tried this experiment tonight, for example, and tomorrow woke up before my alarm, that may be because I needed that amount of sleep or it could be for a bunch of different reasons. Do you do this three nights in a row, or what do you recommend?

Dr. Breus: Usually, seven to 10 days is what it takes because we also want to get the weekends in there. Another important thing is people need to wake up at the same time, even on the weekends. I know that stinks. I know that's not what people want to do. But, if you don't wake up consistently, then you will have an extremely tough time waking up. Something that we call social jet lag occurs.

If you sleep in by even as little as 30 minutes, you're going to end up changing that biological rhythm. It's going to shift, making it very hard to wake up on Monday morning. If you stay up late Friday and sleep in Saturday, stay up late Saturday and sleep in Sunday, come Monday morning, your brain is not going to know what to do. That makes it tough.

Dave: Wow, everyone just closed this book right now because they're not happy reading that. We talked a little bit about dispelling that myth. That's awesome. To be honest, I always thought seven to eight hours is what people needed. When I would meet people who just sleep five hours, I always judged them and thought, "Okay. You're ruining your health and don't even know it."

THE MORE SLEEP, THE BETTER?

Dr. Breus: The evidence is really if you're getting less than six hours a night. If you're somebody who gets five and a half hours of sleep a night, that's where we start to see some of the health effects of sleep deprivation. Now, remember, everybody is different, so it's hard to give a hard and fast rule. The data would suggest that if you sleep five hours or less, or 10 hours or more, that you would have close to a double mortality rate.

Dave: Wow. Can you explain why sleeping more? I would have thought the more sleep, the better.

Dr. Breus: I know, right? That was my first thought, too, "What's going on with this study?" Usually, it turns out that the people who are sleeping more than 10 hours have a sleep quality problem. They have a sleep disorder like sleep apnea or narcolepsy.

Also, we have a very large percentage of people who sleep that much and have a significant amount of depression. When you look at those three factors, they can have a pretty significant effect on your overall health.

THE EFFECTS OF SLEEP DEPRIVATION

Dave: Interesting. Sarah and maybe a ton of other readers right now might be comforted in knowing that the six or seven hours sleep they are getting on an average night is okay and potentially healthy. She does say she sleeps five or maybe six hours. For someone who's getting too little sleep, what are some of the physical manifestations they could potentially see in their life?

Dr. Breus: One of the first things we see with that level of sleep deprivation is your thinking slows down. You're just not making good decisions when you don't have enough sleep. Obviously, we know things like reaction time change quite a bit. It slows by about 30%. You're almost three times slower when you are sleep deprived than when you're not.

That comes into play when you're driving a vehicle, doing something at work that requires machinery, carpooling, something like that. From a cognitive standpoint, you're just fuzzy-headed. You just don't think really straight. Then emotionally, your emotions can be all over the place.

First of all, there's data to suggest that if you're sleeping less than six hours a night, you view things in a more negative light than in a positive light. Second, you have a tendency to be more reactive to those negative emotions. That's where the yelling and the screaming can come in.

Dave: Now, we're talking specifically about people who sleep maybe five hours a night. What about, for example, I consider myself to be someone that needs a lot of sleep. I think I need about eight, eight-and-a-half hours per night. If I was sleeping seven hours, will those same symptoms show up in my life even though I'm still getting more than six hours?

Dr. Breus: It's unlikely, but some people are very sensitive. I can't say never, but I would say there's less of a likelihood.

Dave: Interesting. Now, I know a lot of people are reading this and thinking, "I feel tired all the time," or, "I never feel like I'm getting the quality of sleep that I'm looking for." As The Sleep Doctor, what do you recommend? What can we do to improve the quality of our sleep?

WHAT IS A SLEEP CHRONOTYPE?

Dr. Breus: Well, one of the things I talk about with people all the time is knowing and understanding their chronotype. I just released a book called, *The Power of When*. It's all about telling you when you should do things and understanding your genetic propensity.

It turns out there's a gene called your PER3 gene. The length and the width of the gene determines how much sleep you need, which is what we're discussing now, as well as when you should be sleeping. People always say, "Well, Michael, what's a chronotype? That's a big word. What does that mean?" People have actually heard of chronotypes before but they may not realize it. If you've ever heard of somebody being called an early bird or a night owl... is that a term you've ever heard, Dave?

Dave: Yeah, early bird, night hawk maybe.

Dr. Breus: Right, right. For those people, their genetics are actually making them go to bed earlier and wake up earlier or go to bed later and wake up later. Through my research and working with patients, I discovered there are not just two types. There's actually four different types.

By understanding these four types, I can understand what their hormone distribution level is. Then, I can tell them all kinds of interesting things about themselves. Once you know your chronotype, you know when to go to bed and when to wake up. Once you know that, things get a lot easier.

Dave: You've really piqued my curiosity here because I actually did your chronotype quiz. For all the readers, I'll put a link at the end of this chapter. I did this chronotype quiz, and it asked some very bizarre questions, and then told me that my chronotype is a dolphin. Can you tell me about that? What does that mean?

Dr. Breus: Sure. Like I said before, there are four chronotypes. What I try to do is understand what your chronotype is to give me a reference. Let me go through the four chronotypes, and then I'll go to dolphin last so we can really focus in on you.

Dave: Sure.

LIONS

Dr. Breus: The first one, I replaced early bird with what I call a lion. Lions have a tendency to wake up very early like an early bird would. They'd get up around 5:30, 6 o'clock. These are my CEOs of the world. These are my leaders. These are the people that have a greater tendency to follow their rule.

They usually set up a list every morning, and they check off the list to make sure that they're accomplishing things. Socially, they tend to have a problem. Because they get up so early, they don't like to stay up very late.

These are my people who are going to bed by 9 o'clock, so they're socially missing out on a lot. They may get a lot of stuff done at work with that type-A personality, but they're not really doing a great job on the social side of things. They represent about 15% of the population.

BEARS

Bears represent about 55% of the population. They're the largest group out there. These are my extroverts. These are the people are the glue that keeps society together.

They're very, very interesting people. They do a great job of working hard and playing hard. When you sit down for lunch, you want to sit next to a bear because they're always telling a funny story or they're very gregarious. They're a lot of fun to be around. They're the person to go out to dinner with, that kind of thing.

WOLVES

Then there are my night people who I call wolves. I happen to be a night person myself. I prefer to go to bed around 12:30, 1 o'clock, waking up around 6:30. No actually, like 7:30 if I get my way.

We have a tendency to be more introverted. We are more artistic in nature and creative in nature, so we're authors, musicians, actors, and things like that. We're a little standoffish at first. Society really doesn't like the night person because we're up when everybody else is presumably asleep.

DOLPHINS

The final category is the dolphin. I chose dolphins because in the animal kingdom—most people don't know it—but dolphins sleep unihemispherically, meaning that half of their brain is asleep while the other half is awake and looking for predators. I thought that was a good representation of my people who are not-so-great sleepers.

My dolphins are very intelligent, but one of the things they have a problem with is their perfectionistic side. At times, this perfectionistic side can get in the way of them actually completing tasks.

While they are my type-A personalities as well, they're just not as productive— at least generally speaking—as my lions have a tendency to be. Maybe a little on the neurotic side because they're always looking at different details and things like that. Did I strike a chord with you there, Dave?

Dave: Totally. Yeah, exactly. It started to bring into light why the questions in this quiz were what they are.

Dr. Breus: The first 10 questions help me determine if you're a dolphin. If you make it through that, then you get slotted into either the lion, the bear, or the wolf. I designed my book around all four of the chronotypes.

It seems dolphins get a lot out of it because it teaches them how to schedule their day. Everything from going to bed and your wake-up time, to when you are going to perform best from a productivity standpoint.

When is it good to brainstorm? When is it good to have sex? When is it good to do analysis? When is it good to email, to ask your boss for a raise? These types of things. Throughout the day, you'll find there are certain types of time zones—if you will—that work really well for particular activities. I found that's the case for me and we seem to be getting quite a bit of feedback from the folks reading the book.

SOCIAL SCHEDULES AND SLEEP CHRONOTYPES

Dave: You piqued my curiosity again when you're describing the wolf chronotype. You said that you relate very closely to the wolf.

Dr. Breus: I do.

Dave: They're someone that wants to be awake later in the evening. We've also talked about social sleep schedules and how society isn't built around that schedule. What does someone do when their social schedule doesn't match with their own chronotype? How can you deal with that or can you?

Dr. Breus: That's a tough one. I'll tell you a quick story. I got into this because I had a patient who came to me for insomnia. We were digging around. My techniques, quite frankly, were not working. I couldn't understand why.

Once I started to get more involved in her treatment, she said, "It's not that I can't fall asleep and it's not that I can't stay asleep." She said, "I sleep at the wrong times." So the question becomes, what happens when your body wants to sleep at a time, but the rest of the world doesn't want you to sleep at that time?

She was in quite a bit of distress because she was about to get fired from work. I said, "Can I call your boss and talk to him?" She's like, "You can do whatever you want." I called her boss and said, "We've got a situation here. Would you be willing to let her come in about an hour-and-a-half, two hours later, and stay about an hour-and-a-half, two hours later, just as an experiment?" He said, "I'm like a week away from firing her, and I really like her as a person. I want to see her succeed here, so I'm willing to try anything."

We did the experiment. I called him back in a week. He said, "I don't know what you did to her, but she has changed completely." He said, "She shows up to work at the new time. No problem. She doesn't fall asleep in meetings. Her work product has improved a thousand percent." He said, "This is amazing."

I called her back to give her the news. I got her husband on the phone. I said, "What do you think of what's going on?" He said, "I like my wife more." I thought that was really interesting. Her misalignment with the rest of the world was really making it difficult to have a relationship.

He said, "One of the things that we've discovered is now I know and understand how she works. I know when to talk to her and when not to talk to her."

We use the "power of when" as a methodology for better communication, and that level of communication can be very effective in terms of knowing and understanding when people do things.

Let's say you've got a boss who is just immovable, or you've got a job where you have a shift, and you got to run it. Well, there's actually a section in the book that teaches you how to hack your chronotype. It's a little bit on the complicated side, but it involves light, melatonin, and caffeine. It's perfectly healthy. It's not something that's going to hurt you in the long run, but it's something that you'd have to do fairly frequently.

My best suggestion is for people to educate those around them about their chronotypes. You might be surprised. I've had more employers call me up after one of their employees has read the book and they say, "Wow, can we chronotype me and can we chronotype the rest of my staff?" What he was finding was fascinating. What he was finding was he could actually hold meetings at particular times with certain chronotypes and the meeting was more effective.

Dave: This is so fascinating to me. I'm a big personality type person. I believe Myers-Briggs—or whatever personality typing system you use—tells a lot about work styles and team building. It can be useful in so many different areas. As you're talking about these chronotypes, it's the same thing, just looking through a slightly different lens at how people can work together.

Dr. Breus: Yeah, exactly. I'm now having different companies call me up, and I'm chronotyping their entire company. We're getting everybody to take the quiz. Then we're talking with the managers. We're saying, "You've got this number of wolves, this number of bears, this number of dolphins, and this number of lions. If you're trying to get a task done, these are the best times for these people to hear the instructions for the task. Then these are the best times for them to do certain parts of the task." What we're finding is the productivity levels are increasing dramatically.

Dave: Wow, interesting. You mentioned that bears I think you said are 55% of the population.

Dr. Breus: Correct, yup. That's right.

Dave: Would you say that society then has based itself on a sleep-wake schedule or a work-rest schedule to favor bears?

Dr. Breus: It has, absolutely. There's no question about it. The world is a bear's world—as I like to say—because that's how society has gotten to be because there's so many of them. That's okay because one in two people is a bear. It's just tough for us wolves out there or the lions, or you, as a dolphin. Dolphins can actually work within the schedule once they get their sleep straightened out. Again, the book does a good job of mapping that out for people. They have a tendency to fall in line a little bit easier.

FOLLOW YOUR CHRONOTYPE RHYTHM

Dave: Interesting, interesting. Now, this book is directly about health, but I get a lot of questions about weight-loss and fitness. I'm just wondering if you could speak on that a little bit. Aside from productivity, how can working our chronotype and getting the right sleep affect our weight-loss or fitness level?

Dr. Breus: It depends on what kind of fitness we're talking about. Once you know your chronotype, I teach you what is the perfect time of day to go for a run, as an example. I break it down into cardio—like going for a run—versus non-cardio activities—like weightlifting—because that's a whole different kind of thing, as well as yoga or playing a team sport.

In the book, I actually break these down into four categories, and I give people information surrounding the best time to do those things. Most people like to ask me about the cardio aspect of it because I think there are more people doing cardio than just about anything else. What I'm going to do, if it's okay with you, is talk more from a cardio perspective? Is that fine?

Dave: Yeah, please do.

Dr. Breus: When we look at cardio, you have to decide what it is that you're trying to accomplish. As an example, if you're trying to burn fat with cardio, then exercising more in the morning is going to be better.

Believe it or not, exercising on an empty stomach is actually going to burn more fat than you normally would. Now, I'm not talking about training for a marathon, right? Obviously, you need fuel for that. I'm talking about if you're doing a 20 to 30-minute cardio workout, maybe even 45 minutes.

By the way, I'm not saying not to hydrate. Everybody should hydrate. Literally, the second you wake up in the morning, you should be drinking six to eight ounces— probably eight to 12 ounces to be realistic—of water because your body is breathing out almost a liter of water each night.

If you're trying to lose fat and you're doing it with cardio, it's best to actually exercise in the early morning because that's what's called "the fat burning rhythm." If you have what's called a fasting workout—so, you haven't eaten all night, and you're working out in the morning within a half hour of waking—it actually converts fat into energy because you haven't ingested any carbs yet. Afterward, you would want to eat a breakfast of about 50% carbs and about 50% protein/fat to keep those metabolic fires going.

Let's say that you're not trying to burn fat. Let's say that you're trying to do performance, right? You're trying to do your best run or get your best time. There was a great study in 2015—a British one—and it showed that the most significant factor in predicting athletic peak performance across a wide range of sports is the time that the athletes prefer to rise relative to the time that they perform.

Researchers had athletes train at several different times throughout the day, and then they measured their speed and agility. The early risers—so my lions—actually performed best in the late morning, whereas the intermediate risers—or my bears—did best in the afternoon.

Then the late risers who are my wolves did best in the evenings. So from a performance standpoint, you want to try and follow your chrono rhythm, if at all possible.

There is a worst time to do a run, by the way. That's around 6 am. That's interesting because many people say, "What are you talking about, Michael? That's the only time I have to go for a run." The reason is when you run at dawn, or close to it, you have a very high risk of injury.

Your core body temperature is low. Muscles and joints are really susceptible to strain and tear. If you can wait until 90 minutes after waking up, your core body temperature will have risen. The injury risk drops significantly. With the change in seasons, especially if you're in drier climates, it can be very helpful.

Dave: That is just absolutely fascinating. From a psychological perspective, I often recommend clients to exercise in the morning just because—as you probably have experienced yourself—things get in the way of exercise the later in the day. Exercise gets pushed. It's unfortunate, because psychologically or convenience-wise, I do think it makes sense to exercise in the morning. For some people, that will never be the peak time for them actually to do it.

Dr. Breus: Exactly. It depends on who you're training with, right? If you're working with an elite athlete and that's what they do, well, that's a whole different story. If you're working with somebody like me who's a doctor and is busy seeing patients, trying to get stuff done, I might turn to you and say, "You know what? The only time I have is really at 6 am."

Well, if that's the case, then we really want to make sure we're stretching people out. We're making sure to warm them up to avoid those levels of injury. Quite frankly, there are some people that if you don't exercise them in the morning, they're just not going to do it.

Dave: Exactly, exactly. At least from my perspective of helping people try and get in shape, the most important factor is just doing the exercise. Even if you would actually perform best if you workout in the afternoon and instead you're working out in the morning just to make sure it gets done, I'll take that. Get it done.

Dr. Breus: Right.

Dave: Michael, awesome. Personally, I love the topic of sleep because it's something that I've struggled with over the years, and so I'm really excited to dive into my dolphin chronotype and learn more about it. Thanks for being a part of this interview today, for answering Sarah's question, and for sharing a lot of wisdom. I really appreciate it.

Dr. Breus: No, thank you for having me, Dave. This has been a lot of fun. Thanks everybody for reading.

Dave: Thanks again, Dr. Breus, for being a part of this book and for sharing some really interesting information about sleep. To all the readers, hopefully, you all learned a lot and are eager to try Dr. Breus's test as well.

RESOURCES

Dr. Breus's Website: http://thesleepdoctor.com

Power of When Quiz: http://thepowerofwhenquiz.com

Power of When Book:
http://makeyourbodywork.com/mb-power-of-when

CHAPTER 14:

DO SUPPLEMENTS MAKE A DIFFERENCE?

There's a reason why I saved this interview for last. It's not because supplements are unimportant. Rather, it's because supplements are just that – they *supplement* your healthy lifestyle. They don't *create* a healthy lifestyle.

Stephanie wondered how to put this into practice. She wanted to know which supplements provide the greatest benefit, particularly for losing weight:

> *"For years I've been taking a multivitamin every day, but I've read that they aren't absorbed very well, so it might just be a waste of money altogether. Is this true?*
>
> *Are there other supplements that do offer some sort of benefit that I should consider taking. I don't like the idea of taking all sorts of pills, but I do suspect that my diet doesn't give me everything my body needs.*
>
> *I'm also interested in anything that will help with my metabolism, anything that will help me lose weight. I'm in for it."*

In the previous chapters of this book, we've discussed many strategies you can use to transform your life, your health, and your weight. How can you use supplements as a tool to derive even greater benefits from the healthy choices you are going to make?

MEET DR. PAUL ZICKLER

Dr. Paul Zickler, a medical doctor, has been in practice for over 40 years. He is an expert in natural health and is the Medical Director for YesWellness.com.

Dr. Zickler helps people resolve health issues at their core, avoiding prescription medication whenever possible. First and foremost, his goal is to help his patients prevent disease or illness from ever occurring by implementing the right healthy lifestyle habits.

THE INTERVIEW

Dave: Hey, Paul, thanks so much for joining me in this interview today.

Dr. Zickler: Pleased to be with you.

Dave: We met a couple of weeks ago and were chatting about health and wellness, as well as all different areas of living well. We really had a connection, and I feel like we're on the same page. So I'm excited you had some time for this interview today. Before we dive into today's question, you could tell the readers a little bit about who you are and your long history in the health and wellness industry.

Dr. Zickler: It's a very convoluted history. I started out a long time ago in the emergency department, which I did for 20 years. Then, I followed a career in family practice and urgent care clinics. I'm also an owner of my business, an online pharmacy business, and a founder of YesWellness.com, which is involved with nutraceuticals and supplements. I'm their medical director as of now.

Dave: That's an interesting combination because I know I've met many doctors over the years who stick to either Western medicine or Eastern medicine and rarely do they seem to cross over. As you and I chatted, it sounded like you've bridged the gap and embraced both.

Dr. Zickler: Well, yes. The reason—as I mentioned to you earlier—is that my daughter is a naturopath. While I was working as a family doctor, she was studying to be a naturopath at Bastyr, which is in Seattle just south of us. I took an interest in what their curriculum was. Because as far as I was concerned, they were quacks.

Dave: Thanks for your honesty.

Dr. Zickler: That's what I was told. I took an interest in what she was learning. Then, I attended numerous courses at Bastyr. After the first few, I became very impressed with the naturopath's breadth of knowledge in allopathic medicine. They have an increased knowledge of all the other avenues of medicine, some that I'd never been exposed to. I was fascinated. I began to think outside the box.

Physicians are taught a certain way, and that's the only way. They think with old rhythms. Stepping outside the box is exceedingly hard. But I did it. I started reading literature that wasn't just the New England Journal of Medicine, or JAMA, or the Canadian Journal of Medicine. I looked at alternative medicine and reading some of their research. It opened my eyes and made me realize there is more than one right way.

I am a strong believer in the movement taking place now called holistic or integrated functional medicine because it integrates the best of both worlds. It makes a treatment plan specific to the patient and addresses the root causes of illness rather than just treating your symptoms.

TREATMENTS VERSUS PRESCRIPTIONS: WHICH APPROACH OFFERS REAL SOLUTIONS?

Dave: It was neat. When we met, you told me a story of a patient. I'm sure this happened with tons of your patients, but as you started to explore these alternative medicines, you said you hand-picked your patients. The ones you felt comfortable with to try it out, as opposed to pulling out your prescription pad and writing the typical prescription. Instead, you started to prescribe or recommend some of these alternative medicines. You told me your patient started getting amazing results from this different approach.

Dr. Zickler: That was the case. It's the case physicians who are following integrated functional medicine are seeing as well. Their outcomes are much improved. It's very typical. I started simple, with the common ailment of reflux, or heartburn. The modest solution was just some apple cider vinegar 3 times a day.

The patient had been on medications—what is used in medicine now—the PPIs and histamine blockers. After a period of 2 to 3 weeks, we had the patient off their medication and doing very well with a simple treatment. I was amazed. Then I tried it on a few other of my patients.

As I mentioned to you, I had to pre-select people. Just as I have difficulty discussing some alternative methods with my peers, it's similar to patients; some are ready to accept this kind of alternative information, and others aren't. You quickly realize which ones are and which ones aren't.

The people thinking outside the box—or have the ability to think outside the box—looked at natural or more common methods of reducing their symptoms, as opposed to taking a prescription drug.

As I said, if patients have confidence in their healthcare giver, and you as a healthcare giver are empowering them to look into their health and be part of the process, the results are always much better.

Dave: That's neat because I know there is a movement away from piling on prescription medication on top of prescription medication. But at the same time—and I speak for myself—when someone has a condition they want to be solved, it is tempting to say to a doctor, "Doc, just give me whatever I need to take." But not to trust some of those who are trying out some of the other methods.

Dr. Zickler: That's true, Dave. It's a process. It's a process to empower yourself and your health. It's a lifestyle change. We talked about the motivation of making the decision to take part in your health.

Wellness is based on good nutrition and exercise, along with the harder to describe things. The spiritual, the stress regulators we need in this day and age, and being part of the community. They are all integral parts of making the transition.

You have to buy in. It doesn't happen overnight. That's why it doesn't work for everybody. But if you have a person who has a small interest, having the right approach and showing them step-by-step how to attain it, and then seeing that they're getting the results will help them buy in. Then, you watch their enthusiasm as they become more and more involved.

OUR CHANGING TIMES AND THE IMPACT ON YOUR HEALTH

Dave: I wish we'd recorded the conversation we had a couple of weeks ago because there was so much interesting information I would like to share. I want to go back to one of the points you had made. You were talking about the amount of stress adults today are under is so infinitely greater than stress an adult would have faced 20, 30, 50 years ago. That obviously degrades our health today, but it's something we don't even realize because we're just used to being under stress.

Dr. Zickler: That's true. Look back 50 years ago. My parents are 95, and they were farmers. I can recollect their diet consisted of everything they grew or raised. Their cows and their pigs and their sheep were all raised on grazing.

They produced their own food, sausages, and everything. I remember the butcher coming to butcher everything and making the sausages right there. They worked all day. They were physically active all day, from morning until night, and they were happy. Now compare that to our day today.

Getting up in White Rock at 5:30 in the morning, driving to Vancouver to avoid all the traffic and working at least till 6:00 or 7:00. Then driving with the traffic, and getting home at 8:00 or 9 o'clock at night. Trying to take care of the family, get some exercise, and then try to sleep. On a side not, you've been sitting for most of the day.

So you're creating both an emotional stress, psychological stress, and physical stress. All the stress leads to higher nutrient needs, which we are getting less and less of.

Dave: I love what you are saying. We have higher nutrient needs, but the food we're eating is lower quality.

WHAT'S GONE WRONG WITH OUR FOOD QUALITY?

Dr. Zickler: Yes. Regarding that sort of difference in our lifestyle, you don't have to be a rocket scientist to see the lower food quality has had a significant role in everything ailing us now: our epidemics of diabetes, high blood pressure, as well as dementia and Alzheimer's disease. I am thoroughly convinced it is all stemming from low food quality.

If we look at just the vegetables and the fruits we're eating these days, the vegetables and fruits all look outstanding. They're bigger, juicer, shinier, and absolutely without any blemish. But to get that, they're fed herbicides and pesticides. The nutrients in them are being drawn from a soil that is depleted by over-farming, over-fertilization, relying on fertilizer, not composting, and improper soil management.

Nutrients in the broccoli today, compared to broccoli 50 years ago, are half of what they were. The apple, that beautiful, delicious, large, shiny apple, which is so sweet, is full of a lot more sugar, and a whole pile less pectin. That's our way of life because we have forgotten how our grandparents lived.

Then we go to our meat, dairy, and eggs. You could picture the pastoral scene where the cow is grazing in the field, and the farmer actually knows its name. Eventually, it meets its demise and is butchered for food, and they're respectfully honored for that. Whereas now, we have factory farm animal products.

I think there are 10 billion animals, not counting fish, that were raised in America last year in farms. Most will never see daylight, except on the way to slaughter. They're living in dark, tiny, unsanitary conditions, and diseases spread rapidly. They're given antibiotics and growth hormone. Then their manure is used to fertilize the fields that are already nutrient depleted as well. All those pesticides, herbicides, and things are washed into our water. We're imbibing them on a daily basis.

You can see the world has changed. On top of that, when we hear the doctor say, "Listen, multivitamins? You're probably wasting your money. You should really eat all your greens and vegetables and fruits." That's good advice, except the fruits and vegetables and greens we're supposed to be eating–unless you're getting them from an organic farm, or you're growing them yourself on good soil without pesticides—don't give you what you need. There is a problem here of giving the proper messages to people.

Dave: We are going to get to Stephanie's question, but you've given me so many more questions. You alluded to the fact organics could be the solution. Would you say that? When you talk about the nutrient value in broccoli being half of what it used to be if we were to buy organic broccoli, are we then safe?

Dr. Zickler: We are definitely safer than before. We're still dealing with the same stress and toxic overload regarding environmental toxins we have to deal with. The processed foods we imbibe don't have all the necessary nutrients and use up our stored nutrients to be functional in our body, which depletes our cells. Yes, the organic broccoli in itself is a much better choice.

My suggestion is to buy your vegetables organically. You can go online to get the *dirty dozen*, the ones that you really want to avoid and make sure are organic. Those would be much safer. But you still have to deal with all the other factors as well. Similarly, if you can't afford to buy organic vegetables and fruits, by all means, still eat vegetables and fruits.

Dave: I'm glad you made that message.

Dr. Zickler: Similarly, if you are a meat eater, make sure your meat is grass fed, pasture fed, and without any additives like antibiotics and growth hormone. Eat meat in a balanced way with your fruits and vegetables. Then you're on your way to a better wellness.

ARE YOUR PORTION SIZES BASED ON WHAT YOUR BODY ACTUALLY NEEDS?

Dave: I like that you mentioned eating grass fed meat. That's something I get asked a lot about because it is so much more expensive. Particularly, beef prices right now are just through the roof. If you throw in grass fed in there, it makes it even worse. But one thing that I always encourage people to think about is their portion sizes.

Somehow, over the years we've developed this notion we're always protein deficient and need huge meat portion sizes. When reducing your portion size by about half, you're still getting the protein you need, and you're cutting down your food bill in a huge way.

Dr. Zickler: You're absolutely correct. When I look at our own food, I think of buying one of those big dollar size pieces of beef tenderloin that are grass fed. It's delicious, and it's about all I need. I get that maybe once every 2 weeks, and rely on other sources for protein as well. So your point is well taken. I think your meat sources, whether they be poultry or fish or meat, the size of a deck of cards is about a meal size.

Dave: That's such a good rule of thumb for people to use. We all know what a deck of cards looks like. Use that as your portion size. Then think about, I think it's comical. When I look at chicken breasts, they're like 2 or 3 decks of cards. I just think, there's no way that the majority of people are only eating a third of this chicken breast. We all just eat a whole chicken breast.

Dr. Zickler: Yes, exactly. That's another thing that's changed over the last 50 years. The fact that plate sizes are bigger. When I look at some of my mom and dad's old plates, they're not nearly as big as our plates. When you take that and add the portion of vegetables, you see that a significant amount of their plate was covered with vegetables.

If it were summertime, there'd be all different colors of vegetables, from radishes to white radishes, to broccoli, to peppers. The wintertime was full of root vegetables, which are different colors. They had turnips, parsnips, beets, and other things they could store. It was so much different in terms of what they're putting inside their body.

WHAT ARE SUPPLEMENTS GOOD FOR?

Dave: I want to use that as a transition to what Stephanie asked. I liked her question because she is understands something is missing from her diet. She doesn't elaborate whether she's talking about food quality or if she's not getting a balanced array of fruits and vegetables. But she says, "I get it. My diet isn't complete. But should I even spend my money or my time going out and getting supplements, and if so, which ones?" When you read that, what's your instant reaction? Or what have you told past patients of yours when it comes to vitamins?

Dr. Zickler: Well, I think all the aforementioned things we talked about—nutrition and exercise, and being emotionally and mentally healthy—are the important, basic things. Once we do that 80% of the time, then you can think about adding supplements.

I don't want people to think, "I'm going to lead my life the way it is, and I'm going to add all these vitamins and supplements, and it's going to fix everything." That's not what's going to happen. They're barking up the wrong tree.

We want to get their core of their health in good order, and then enhance that with vitamins and supplements. We discussed the need for supplementing with our diet. But as we work to make our diet healthier and make ourselves healthier, the need for supplements is not as necessary.

Dave: Just thinking about the name, they're supplements. I know I sometimes forget what that actually means? It's just like you just said, they're intended to supplement a healthy diet and healthy lifestyle.

Dr. Zickler: Right. Regarding what advice I would give them, I would start with a good multivitamin. A good multivitamin would be one that is whole food based. I say go to London Drugs. You'll see a whole 3 rows of vitamin A and 3 rows of vitamin B. They're all in alphabetical order. People are buying 1 of this, 1 of that, and 1 of another. Instead of buying a product made from whole foods, which has all those elements in it. But it also has all the co-factors, co-enzymes, antioxidants, and other things we haven't discovered yet that make them work together, synergistically.

Often times I see naturopaths fall in the same pitfalls as the allopathic doctor with his prescriptions. You get a list of all these vitamins you're going to buy every week, when really what you need to do is incorporate it into a whole food kind of package. That's what I would suggest. Vitamin D3 and fish oil. I think those are the very least you should start with.

Once you've got good control over your wellness, you can add other ones specific to your unique needs with a good healthcare provider. If you're a runner, you may need more. If you're under a lot of stress and multiple strategies for dealing with your stress haven't worked, there might be other supplements that deal specifically more with stress.

If you have difficulty sleeping, there might be some which help. You might be doing all the right things, but you could need a little enhancement. There are core supplements, and then there are supplements you need to use to enhance certain things you want enhanced.

THE PROBLEM WITH SYNTHETIC SUPPLEMENTS

Dave: Can you comment on Stephanie's question about multivitamins or supplements aren't absorbed and therefore, we pee out the supplements. What's your perspective on that? Do supplements actually work?

Dr. Zickler: Yes. That's again going back to real versus synthetic. A lot of multivitamins are synthetically produced. They package the individual synthetic components, and often in much higher doses than we need. You'll see you have fluorescent yellow pee because the vitamin B complex is all being peed out. As opposed to a multivitamin that is whole food origins and has all the other added things I alluded to which helps absorbs what you need.

A lot of the information we get is multivitamins aren't necessary. We've certainly discussed the reasons for or the need for multivitamins.

DR. ZICKLER'S RECOMMENDED MULTIVITAMINS

Dave: Yeah, for sure. Now, I want to go through the other two you just mentioned but you said to start off with your basics; you need a good quality multi. Is there a specific multi that you recommend? I know the readers would probably be interested to hear. Is there a brand? A specific one?

Dr. Zickler: Rather than say one specific brand, there are several that are very good. What you want to look for is a natural vitamin as close as possible to its natural form. Make sure utmost care has been taken in all phases of its production, from growing its ingredients to manufacturing, testing for potency, and quality control. Make sure you speak to a healthcare provider or find a reliable website to ensure the information is accurate.

If you don't want to do all that kind of research, pick well-known and professional producers. They are more likely to have the most beneficial product. Look at companies that have a long track record of providing really high-quality products producing good clinical results. That would be my suggestion.

Dave: Sorry, I'm going to push you on it a little bit more. Are there specific brands then? Because I'll speak for myself: I don't know which brands have a long history of providing good quality products. Could you point me in the right direction?

Dr. Zickler: Some of the ones we sell are Douglas Labs, Thorne, Sisu. But there are some professional brands out there which are equally as good if you follow my instructions.

Dave: That's helpful. What I'll do for the readers is I'll link out to the three multivitamin manufacturers in the *Resources* section at the end of this chapter. And like Dr. Zickler's recommending, see what information is available on those, and then make an informed decision. This gives us a start.

VITAMIN D3 AND FISH OIL RECOMMENDATIONS

The next question I had for you was about D3. What's the rationale behind most people benefiting from a D3 supplement? How does this supplement work?

Dr. Zickler: A group of people started working in a research lab, looking at deficiencies and why people were getting sick. Vitamin D sort of came up on the radar. Looking at a lot of data and diseases, they found people were deficient in vitamin D. Once that was changed, the likelihood of eliminating the deficiency was much greater.

That research exploded on vitamin D3, and D3 is the most active one. Don't get D2. D3 is especially important because it is produced by yourself, through the sun. But especially for us people in a temperate climate, we're not exposed to enough sun. Let's just get back to the natural, the sun producer of vitamin D3.

If you expose at least 40% of your body to the sun for at least 20 minutes, or enough to get a light red tinge on your skin, that should be adequate for you to get enough vitamin D3 produced all by yourself.

The problem is we can't do that all year round. From about late October to May, we're not getting nearly enough sun to produce the vitamin D we need. That's where a supplement is required. The supplement is very easy to take. The only problem is a lot of these suggested conventional requirements are way too low.

I think the food guide suggests taking 400 international units now, which is way too low. For adults, I think it should be in the neighborhood of 4,000-6,000. If you have darker skin, it's closer to 6-8,000. The run of the mill dosage is between 4 and 6,000 units a day.

A year ago, Health Canada changed their marketing for vitamin D, so you can't get a stronger product than 1,000 mg. They used to have 5,000 mg, which would be great. But now they're only 1,000 international units. I suggest getting the vitamin D in oil. One drop is 1,000 international units. So taking 5 drops a day is a piece of cake, as opposed to the big tablets.

Dave: That's really helpful. That's something I don't take. I would have assumed taking a multivitamin would get my vitamin D in an adequate dosage, so it's interesting to hear you say that's not the case.

Dr. Zickler: Most multivitamins won't have that high dosage in their compendium.

Dave: Then the third one you mentioned was fish oil. Why would most people benefit from taking a high-quality fish oil?

Dr. Zickler: Fish oils, being polyunsaturated fats, specifically DHE, DHA, and EPH, are required free fatty acids for multiple reasons. One of them is neurological. The neurons and the brain are made up primarily of fats.

These are required for both neurological and brain health. It's important—to prevent Alzheimer's and dementia—your free fatty acids are adequate. They are involved in multiple other metabolic issues too, such as immune protection and general good metabolism.

Dave: That's super helpful. This is for Stephanie and anyone else who had a similar question about if these supplements are worthwhile. To recap: a good quality multi comes from good whole food sources. Regarding D3, we're looking for a higher dosage than most will come in, in Canada at least. Again, in the *Resources* section, I'll link out to the brands Dr. Zickler recommends.

Dr. Zickler, thanks again so much for your time today, for sharing your expertise, and particularly for sharing some practical steps people can use today. Thanks for being in this interview.

Dr. Zickler: You're very welcome. I enjoyed it.

RESOURCES

Dr. Zickler's Website: https://www.yeswellness.com/

The Dirty Dozen and the Clean Fifteen: http://makeyourbodywork.com/dirty-dozen-clean-15

Dr. Zickler's Recommended Multivitamins:
http://makeyourbodywork.com/pz-douglas-multi
http://makeyourbodywork.com/pz-thorne-multi
http://makeyourbodywork.com/pz-sisu-multi

Dr. Zickler's Recommended D3 Drops: http://makeyourbodywork.com/pz-vitamin-d

Dr. Zickler's Recommended Fish Oil Supplement:
http://makeyourbodywork.com/pz-fish-oil

CONCLUSIONS AND NEXT STEPS

You made it!

How are you feeling after reading the advice from our panel of experts? Excited? Empowered? Maybe a bit overwhelmed?

In the introduction of this book I offered two guidelines to keep in mind as you began reading:

> 1. *It's impossible to do everything at once.*

> 2. *You can begin today.*

I would now like you to take action on what you've just read and learned. Don't try to do everything. Start with one thing. Start today.

What will it be for you?

If you're not sure what your first step will be, I strongly urge you to work your way through the *Can't Lose Workbook* that you may have purchased along with this book. If you need a copy, go to http://makeyourbodywork.com/cant-lose-workbook.

Sometimes it's helpful to have a professional walk you through the steps needed to make positive change. In this book, you've been introduced to 14 such professionals, and have been provided with their contact information at the end of each chapter. I know they would love to hear from you.

And, I'm here to help too! Feel free to contact me any time via email: dave@makeyourbodywork.com.

ABOUT THE AUTHOR

 Dave Smith is a Certified Personal Trainer and Life Coach who has been helping people reach their health and fitness goals since 2001. The success of his clients has earned Dave international recognition and led to his selection as "Canada's Top Fitness Professional" in 2013.

Dave specializes in helping others develop mastery over simple, step-by-step habits that allow them to effectively lose weight and keep it off for the long-term. More importantly however, he aims to help his clients build confidence and find joy in healthy living. He believes this joy is something everyone can and should experience in life. It's never out of reach.

In addition to coaching clients, Dave hosts a weekly health and wellness podcast called *Make Your Body Work*. He also writes for many print and online magazines, acts as a motivational speaker, and has appeared as a health expert on numerous TV shows. You can learn more and connect with Dave at http://makeyourbodywork.com.